Scandalous Britain

TOM QUINN

Scandalous Britain

TOM QUINN

A History of Notorious Britain:
From the Disreputable and the Seedy
to the Nefarious and the Lascivious

NEW
HOLLAND

First published in 2005 by New Holland Publishers (UK) Ltd
London • Cape Town • Sydney • Auckland

www.newhollandpublishers.com

Garfield House, 86–88 Edgware Road, London W2 2EA, United Kingdom

80 McKenzie Street, Cape Town 8001, South Africa

14 Aquatic Drive, Frenchs Forest, NSW 2086, Australia

218 Lake Road, Northcote, Auckland, New Zealand

10 9 8 7 6 5 4 3 2 1

ISBN 1 84330 967 X

Publishing Manager: Jo Hemmings
Senior Editor: Kate Michell
Assistant Editor: Kate Parker
Copyeditor: Sarah Larter
Design: Adam Morris and Alan Marshall
Indexer: Dorothy Frame
Production: Joan Woodroffe

Reproduction by Pica Digital Pte Ltd, Singapore
Printed and bound in Singapore by Kyodo Printing Co. (Singapore) Pte Ltd

Photographs appearing on the cover are as follows:
Front cover (clockwise from top left): Lord Lucan, John Wilkes, Christine Keeler,
a cockfight, Nell Gwyn, Oscar Wilde and Lord Douglas, Guy Burgess, Aleister
Crowley and Ruth Ellis.
Spine: Ruth Ellis

Introduction

Aristocratic Antics
The Upper-class Underworld

Beyond the Pale
Infamous Eccentrics and Academics

Artistic Licence
Scandals of Bohemia

Masterminds, Murderers and Misers 92
Fraudsters and Freaks

Clerics with Red Faces 120
Irreverent Reverends and Vice-Ridden Vicars

Licentious London
Where Not to be Seen

130

The Political World
Westminster's Seedy Side

144

Outrageous Royals 178
Kinky Kings and Pouting Princesses

Women Behaving Badly 198
Madams and Mistresses

Introduction

A Long History

The writer George Orwell (1903–50) once commented that the British love a really juicy murder. He might also have remarked that the only thing the British love more than a good murder is a really good scandal. Of course, scandal takes many forms – from relatively dry political situations to full-blown sexual affairs. It's better still if a sexual misdemeanour comes complete with royalty, aristocracy, celebrity or espionage.

The juiciest gossip involves the rich and famous, as the rest of us delight in seeing the high and mighty take a tumble, particularly if their fall from grace stems from some ill-considered act in their private lives. Losing your position because you failed at your job is not half as interesting as being swept into the wilderness because you have slept with the wrong person or even several wrong people – preferably at the same time.

The kiss-and-tell story is now commonplace and the newspapers print more or less what they like, but scandal itself isn't a recent phenomenon. It has a

long history, which is tied up with power and position. It is a history that takes us back to the days before radio, television and newspapers to a time when scandals in high places were so damaging that when they were exposed they became lodged in the historic consciousness never to be forgotten. The scandalous behaviour of today's footballers and rock stars will soon fade, but will the world ever forget the scandal surrounding the arrest, trial and imprisonment of Oscar Wilde (see pages 71–3) or the abdication of Edward VIII (see pages 191–5)?

The great scandals of the past conceal a wealth of lesser, but no less fascinating, affronts to society's dignity that caused mayhem at the time, and it is the best – or worst – of these that are collected here. From Edward II's plainly homosexual relationship with Piers Gaveston in late medieval England (see pages 180–81) to the downfall of any number of Conservative politicians in the late-20th century, this is a veritable feast of the best of British scandal.

9.0

Aristocratic Antics –
The Upper-class Underworld

'Much wine had passed,
with grave discourse
Of who fucks who, and who
does worse'
John Wilmot, 2nd Earl of Rochester

A Restoration Rake
John Wilmot, 2nd Earl of Rochester

Even by the somewhat immoral standards of the British aristocracy, John Wilmot, 2nd Earl of Rochester (1647–80) stands out as a shining example of just how scandalous it is possible to be if you really put your mind to it. The idea that he might become the most notorious man of his age could not have been contemplated as the quiet and apparently studious Rochester grew up on the family estate at Ditchley in Oxfordshire. He went to school in Burford, a pretty market town about 20 miles from Oxford, which still looks much as it would have done when Rochester knew it.

Rochester was a good scholar, but by the age of 12, when he was admitted to Wadham College, Oxford, things had started to go wrong. According to accounts of his life written much later, Rochester began a life of debauchery that eventually made him a byword for immorality. His father, Henry (c. 1612–58), had not set a good example for the young man. Created earl in 1652 by the exiled Charles II (1660–85) as a reward for his support of the Royalist cause during the English Civil War, he was a heavy drinker who died abroad when his son was just 11 years old. In today's world, where psychoanalysis creeps into everything, no doubt the behaviour and death of Rochester's father would be used to explain Rochester's apparent change of character.

After leaving Oxford at the age of 14, the younger Rochester began a life that alternated between short periods spent in the country, during which

BELOW: *JOHN WILMOT LIKED A DRINK OR TWO.*

he was relatively sober, and longer periods at court in London, during which he indulged in every vice possible. He was already writing verse by this time, but it was merely to amuse friends and to impress those who mattered.

During his exile in France, Charles II had developed an intense dislike for any religious outlook that denied pleasure, a reaction no doubt to the Puritanical rule of Oliver Cromwell (1599–1658) during the Commonwealth. After his return to England to take the throne in 1660, the king encouraged his young, amusing and often outrageous friends such as Rochester to do exactly as they pleased, and with royal sanction there was little the outraged clergy, or anyone else for that matter, could do.

The Provocative Poet

The Restoration period that followed Charles II's accession was a time that was unmatched in its rejection of conventional morality until the 1960s. Of course, a life of uninterrupted pleasure was only available to the rich and aristocratic, but the period spawned a huge number of plays and books – a whole artistic culture in fact – that would have been impossible at any other time before the 20th century. The Restoration play was typically amoral, cynical, sardonic and irreligious. Its central values were those of the court, where wit and success were prized above all other things. And, in terms of wit, Rochester excelled, but it also got him into trouble when he circulated the following verse among his friends at court.

I' th' isle of Britain, long since famous grown
For breeding the best cunts in Christendom,
There reigns, and oh! long may he reign and thrive,
The easiest King and best-bred man alive.
Him no ambition moves to get renown.
Like the French fool, that wanders up and down
Starving his people, hazarding his crown.
Peace is his aim, his gentleness is such,
And love he loves, for he loves fucking much.

According to one report, Rochester accidentally placed a copy of the poem in the king's hands. Charles was furious and the earl was forced to beat a hasty retreat to Oxfordshire where, presumably bored on one occasion, he set himself up as a quack doctor, trundling around local villages in a cart and offering cures for everything from gout to impotence. Another story tells that he pretended to be a tinker, collecting villagers' pots and pans and then breaking them all.

There was a world-weary edge to Rochester's most cynical verse, and critics have even detected a longing for the sort of religious certainties that, on the face of it, he had rejected outright. His most famous poem, *A Satire Against Reason and Mankind* reveals his loathing of man's conviction that he is somehow superior to the rest of creation.

> *Were I (who to my cost already am*
> *One of those strange, prodigious creatures, man)*
> *A spirit free to choose, for my own share,*
> *What case of flesh and blood I pleased to wear,*
> *I'd be a dog, a monkey or a bear,*
> *Or anything but that vain animal*
> *Who is so proud of being rational.*

But the verse for which Rochester was renowned was more likely to resemble this fragment, which is taken from *The Imperfect Enjoyment*.

> *Naked she lay, clasped in my longing arms,*
> *I filled with love, and she all over charms;*
> *Both equally inspired with eager fire,*
> *Melting through kindness, flaming in desire.*
> *With arms, legs, lips close clinging to embrace,*
> *She clips me to her breast, and sucks me to her face.*
> *Her nimble tongue, Love's lesser lightening, played*
> *Within my mouth, and to my thoughts conveyed*
> *Swift orders that I should prepare to throw*
> *The all-dissolving thunderbolt below.*

And despite his repeated banishment from court, he could never quite leave the king alone, writing, on another occasion:

> *Here sits our good and gracious king*
> *Whose word no man relies on*
> *Who never said a stupid thing*
> *Nor ever did a wise one.*

Worn out with drink and debauchery – and almost certainly suffering from syphilis – Rochester died aged just 34. He is said to have repented his licentious life and been received into the Church on his deathbed – a book was published to this effect soon after he died. However, some believe that this was just another example of Rochester playing a part and amusing himself.

By the end of the 17th century, the moral tone began to change in Britain, almost certainly as a result of the Establishment's revulsion at the lives of

Rochester and his contemporaries. When Charles II died, the rakes' protector was gone, and the royal court took on a far more sombre air.

However, Rochester's scandalous legacy lived on and until the 1960s no complete unexpurgated texts of his work were available anywhere!

The Debauched Dilettanti
Sir Francis Dashwood and the Hellfire Club

The creation of the Hellfire Club seems to have been an extreme example of the 18th-century passion for clubs of all kinds. It was set up by Sir Francis Dashwood (1708–81), the son of a wealthy businessman, as a subversive alternative to the gentlemen's clubs that were opening all over London at the time.

As a young man, Dashwood embarked on the traditional grand tour around Europe and, although he adored the classical art and architecture of Italy, he developed an intense dislike of Catholicism. He married into the aristocracy and eventually became a Member of Parliament, sitting in the House of Commons for more than 20 years. However, he seems to have been attracted to all sorts of oddball organizations. He clearly enjoyed secrecy – he is said to have been a Jacobite secret agent working on behalf of the exiled Charles Edward Stuart (although this seems somewhat at odds with his hatred of Catholicism) – and he is known to have joined the Freemasons and attended a number of black masses. This appears to have given him a taste for the sort of secretive rituals that are supposed to have taken place at the Hellfire Club.

Everything about the Hellfire Club is odd – for a start, during Dashwood's own lifetime it was never in fact known as the Hellfire Club. The idea of the organization was to mimic and mock the more serious rituals of the Catholic Church. The club had its roots in the Society of the Dilettanti, formed by Dashwood in 1736 and which seems to have concentrated on supplying large quantities of women and alcohol to its members. The Society of Dilettanti eventually became the Order of the Friars of St Francis, later known as the Hellfire Club.

In 1751, Dashwood took the lease on Medmenham Abbey, a 12th-century monastery in Buckinghamshire, which he converted into a house and then remodelled in the Gothic manner. Ominously he carved the words 'Do as thou will' above the front door, a motto that was taken very much to heart by the club's members, who called themselves the 'Monks of Medmenham' or the 'Friars of St Francis of Wycombe'. The garden of the abbey had a number of statues that gave clues as to the real purpose of the club – prominently displayed were a naked statue of Venus bending over and a large statue of Priapus in his traditional erect pose!

ABOVE: *Underneath West Wycombe Hill are a network of caves where the Order of the Friars of St Francis – the Hellfire Club – held their unusual gatherings.*

The Club Within The Caves

Underneath West Wycombe hill, on which the abbey stood, was a network of caves, which Dashwood extended so that the 'friars' could meet in even greater secrecy. From the start, London society believed that when the men met under the hill they indulged in every conceivable vice, including drinking, animal sacrifice and orgies.

Small caves were hollowed out so that individual members could entertain their guests in private, and there was a large cave known as the Banqueting Hall. A stream, which eventually became known as the River Styx – the river from classical mythology that led to the underworld – wound through the caves. Across the stream, members could reach another cave, which was known as the Inner Sanctum. It was here that devil worship and black masses were said to take place. In fact, it is far more likely that the members simply gathered together here to get drunk and argue about politics, women and court intrigue.

Whatever the truth about the rumoured satanic rituals, Dashwood's club certainly outraged his contemporaries, but with his huge wealth he cared nothing for the opinions of others. The 18th century was a time when the classical world was particularly admired; houses were built in the classical style and Greek and Roman literature were central to an Englishman's education. Dashwood simply took the whole thing one step further by emulating what he saw as the freedom and liberty of the ancient world. In the caves at West Wycombe there is no doubt that the rich and powerful of the time did as they pleased with an endless stream of prostitutes who were brought up from London. They also enjoyed bouts of drinking that lasted for days and took the opportunity to say what they pleased about some of the country's most cherished institutions – one of the club's strictest rules was that nothing said in the caves must ever be repeated outside.

No one knows exactly when the organization became known as the Hellfire Club, but it was certainly after Dashwood's death in 1781. We know, too, that the members of the club included a wide range of Establishment figures. Thomas Potter, the son of the archbishop of Canterbury; the artist, William Hogarth; the Earl of Bute; Horace Walpole; the Prince of Wales and even Benjamin Franklin, who went on to sign the Declaration of American Independence, were all members.

Forbidden Fruit
Henry Cecil, 10th Earl of Exeter

When the 10th Earl of Exeter (1754–1804) fell in love with a Shropshire farmer's daughter towards the end of the 18th century his family probably thought nothing of it. As members of one of the great aristocratic English families they would probably have assumed that he would make the girl his mistress and then discard her with a payoff when he grew tired of her. None could have imagined what was really about to happen, for the earl was so smitten by humble Sarah Hoggins that he was not content to make her merely his mistress – he wanted to make her his wife. And that's exactly what he did.

By today's standards the story seems immensely romantic – the earl was heir to a vast fortune and to one of England's greatest houses. He had already been married once, but he was so taken with Miss Hoggins that against the objections of the whole family he went ahead and married her. His justification for the marriage – if justification were needed – was that she was exceedingly beautiful and he was in love with her. It was as simple as that. The earl even commissioned one of the greatest portrait painters of the age – Sir Thomas Lawrence (1769–1830) – to paint a huge portrait of him and his new wife. The painting still hangs in the Billiard Room at Burghley House.

Upsetting the Natural Order

The sense of outrage at this blatant attempt to overthrow the usual social order was so great that even those who might have been assumed to support the marriage – including those from Sarah's own background – were equally dismayed, and Sarah was considered to have made a bad marriage simply because she had married out of her class. Little is known about Sarah, even today, and her past as a humble farmer's daughter was kept as quiet as possible once she had assumed her new life as the Countess of Exeter.

But time heals everything and what had once been a great scandal had become the epitome of romance towards the end of the 19th century, as one anonymous writer explained:

It was in the days when George III was king that it happened. The nephew and heir of the then Earl of Exeter, Mr Henry Cecil, was in his youth a gambler, and had undoubtedly a bad wife (though a very beautiful one – Emma Vernon), for he divorced her in 1791. After these losses of money and wife, his uncle, Lord Exeter, advised him to go and live quietly for some time in the country. Mr Cecil followed his advice, and went to live at a small inn at Bolas, in a retired part of Shropshire, but disliking his abode, he went to lodge at a farm-house. Here, the world forgetting, by the world forgot, he remained two years. The farmer had a lovely daughter of 17, who was as good, as pure and gentle as she was beautiful. Mr Cecil had had enough of fashionable ladies, and fell in love with this sweet rustic beauty. He asked her in marriage of her father. She loved him and they were wedded.

Sarah became known as the 'Cottage Countess', and her marriage to the 10th Earl of Exeter was celebrated in the ballad *The Lord of Burghley* by Alfred, Lord Tennyson (1809–92). She died at the age of 24 having given birth to three children.

Going to the Dogs
Francis Henry Egerton, 8th Earl of Bridgewater

A small man with a delicate constitution, Francis Henry Egerton, 8th Earl of Bridgewater (1756–1829) was born into a family wealthy enough to ensure that he never had to work. As an adult he went everywhere accompanied by two huge lackeys who walked one on each side of him, and to make sure that he went unrecognized he wore an enormous sugarloaf hat that was pulled well down over his eyes.

Egerton was always extraordinarily polite to people. If he borrowed a book he insisted on returning it to the owner in his finest carriage. The owner of the book would hear a knock at the door and open it to discover a magnificent landau, four footmen in full livery – and the book they had lent Egerton.

The strange, reclusive figure of Egerton was talked about endlessly. It was reported that he had something to conceal and had been embroiled in some dreadful scandal. Tongues started to wag, and speculation produced rumours that were passed on as fact. Egerton's outrageous lifestyle didn't help. A great lover of dogs, he would sometimes travel on foot while his carriage conveyed a dozen of his favourite pooches. He worried terribly about the state of their feet – although they hardly ever walked anywhere – and scandalized London society when he paid a shoemaker to make boots for them all. But Egerton had a thing about boots – he wore a new pair himself every day, and when he took them off at night he lined them up in perfect rows. No one else was ever allowed to touch them. He took great pleasure in judging how a year had passed by observing the wear and tear on his footwear.

Every day his vast and magnificent dining table was laid for a dozen guests, but no one was ever invited to the house – such were the rumours about Egerton that it is doubtful peole would have come even if he'd invited them. But Egerton didn't care – he preferred to dine with his dogs, so that's exactly what he did every day. Each of his canine companions was provided with a napkin that was fixed on its collar, and each had a servant standing behind ready to wait on it. Apparently the dogs had grown so used to all this that they behaved very well. If they did misbehave they were banished for a day or more to the kitchen and a diet of bread and water.

Animal Lover Extraordinaire
Charles Waterton

Charles Waterton (1782–1865) was the 27th Lord of Walton Hall in Yorkshire, an estate ten miles from Wakefield. Towards the end of his life, few people visited him, so unconventional had his life become. He was considered the most scandalous aristocrat in Britain, as a result of his complete rejection of the traditions and pastimes of his class. His appearance was as odd as his lifestyle. He was variously described as looking like a spider after a long winter's hibernation or like someone recently discharged from prison. He wore such shabby clothes that he was often mistaken for a vagrant or a farm worker. On formal occasions he wore a dark blue, brass-buttoned, swallow-tailed coat that he had worn at school and which was decades out of fashion. Visitors to Walton Hall who rose early frequently spotted him running barefoot about his heavily wooded estate, stopping now and then to climb a tree at incredible speed.

The Aristocratic Animal Sanctuary

To the astonishment of neighbouring farmers and landowners he refused to chop down trees on his estate, however old or decayed they might be, because he believed – quite rightly – that they provided an excellent habitat for birds and insects. In an age when every decent English gentleman enjoyed hunting, fishing and shooting, Waterton refused to allow any creature on his 300-acre estate to be molested in any way. Polite society was aghast. In one incident, Waterton's neighbour Sir George Pilkington proudly showed him a raven he had just shot – he was particularly pleased because he thought it was probably the last such bird in Yorkshire. Waterton was furious and denounced Pilkington to his face as a scoundrel.

Waterton once described in a letter to his sister how he had seen neither a bird nor an animal of any kind on the long road from Walton Hall to Leeds – they had all been shot or trapped by the local people. He believed it was only in his own grounds that the sound of birdsong could be heard. But if the park was packed with birds and animals, the house itself was even more densely populated by wildlife specimens. Many of these objects were collected by Waterton during his travels around South America as a young man. They tended to be stuffed or preserved in Waterton's own liquid concoctions. His clothes were curiously stiff because he continually immersed them in biochloride of mercury, one of the substances he used to protect his natural history specimens from the ravages of moths, mites and bad weather. His collection included monkeys, rare birds and even a full-size crocodile.

Waterton also showed compassion to his fellow humans. So moved was he by the plight of the native Indians on a trip to South America in 1816 that he managed, with the help of some Jesuit friends, to arrange an audience with the Pope to discuss the matter. However, having arrived in Rome, he climbed to the top of a statue in the Vatican and left his gloves there as a memento.

ABOVE: *Charles Waterton was an aristocratic naturalist, who abandoned polite society preferring the company of wildlife and nature. In this unusual portrait he is seen holding a bird and is accompanied by a stuffed cat's head.*

The Pope was indignant and Waterton's audience was cancelled.

But Waterton was always full of surprises. Halfway through dinner he might decide to stand on his head. Or he would demonstrate, usually to distinguished visitors, the benefits of being double-jointed by sitting through a meal with his foot firmly wedged behind his ear. The animals he so adored also influenced his behaviour. When showing visitors around his house, Waterton would occasionally spring up and swing for minutes at a time from a richly carved doorframe. Friends who visited the house regularly became quite used to seeing him in this position, testing out the techniques of the monkeys he had spent so long studying. Such eccentricities made Waterton infamous in his own lifetime, although he was also celebrated for his achievements, most notably the publication of his book *Wanderings in South America* in 1826.

The Nondescript

Tall and very thin with close-cropped hair, Waterton often appeared to be in a state of intense concentration. Although he was a serious naturalist, he also had a humorous side to his personality. For example, some of his taxidermic creations were deliberately designed to fool the gullible and amuse himself. His most famous object was a goblin-like creature called the Nondescript, which was made from a howler monkey's backside, and given piercing eyes and a curious, almost grinning mouth! It was apparently modelled on the features of a tax inspector who had impounded Waterton's specimens at Liverpool on his final return from South America!

By 1826, Waterton had been rejected by society for his behaviour for so long that he decided to block the world out by building a wall round his estate. The final straw in society's eyes came when Waterton married the daughter of a South American tribeswoman. After that, his contemporaries saw it as no real surprise when he then began to invite inmates from the local lunatic asylum to visit the house.

A Public Attraction

Eventually, Waterton opened the estate parkland to visitors – 17,000 people came to Walton Hall every year during the 1840s. He charged no fee but stipulated that no one should enter the park with a dog or a gun. Few visitors would have believed that the ragged, wizened and often shoeless man wandering about the estate was in fact the owner. They often asked him for directions to the lord's house and tipped him a penny, something that delighted him.

Waterton's oddities grew daily. He would crawl under the table and bite his guests' ankles at dinner or hop along the topmost wall of his grotto – a considerable height – on one leg with the other hanging over the chasm. He even made himself a pair of wings and began to consider the possibility of flying from the roof of a barn.

At the age of 80 he was still climbing 60-foot trees with his pockets full of nuts, berries and other titbits for the birds, and he would still show visitors how he could scratch the back of his head with his foot. After an apparently minor fall in the park in May 1865, Waterton's health declined. Three days later he was dead. It is said that a flock of birds followed the cortège as his funeral barge moved slowly across his lake to the island where he was buried.

ABOVE: *THE RIGHT HONOURABLE SIR GERALD HUGH TYRWHITT WILSON, 14TH LORD BERNERS, WAS EXTREMELY ARTISTIC. HE COMPOSED, WROTE AND PAINTED, BUT, MORE FAMOUSLY, HE DYED HIS FLOCKS OF DOVES DIFFERENT COLOURS AMONG OTHER ECCENTRIC ACTIVITIES.*

ABOVE: *The eccentric squire John Mytton squandered his inheritance on mad escapades, such as riding a bear into a party.*

ABOVE LEFT: *George Gordon, Lord Byron, had an incestuous affair with his half-sister.*

RIGHT: *Cult leader Aleister Crowley (1875–1947), a self-confessed sex and drug fiend, was given the title of 'The Wickedest Man In the World' by the British media.*

'Mad, Bad and Dangerous to Know'
George Gordon, Lord Byron

George Gordon, Lord Byron (1788–1824) was undoubtedly the most reviled poet of the early 19th century, when scandalous behaviour became almost mandatory for poets and their ilk. We may now view Byron as simply a great poet and a central figure in the great flowering of Romantic literature at the beginning of the 19th century, but during his lifetime his huge popularity was quickly eclipsed, in England at least, by the details of his debauched private life. Respectable people forbade their daughters even to mention his name, and to read his works was to invite eternal damnation. He was most famously described by one of his mistresses, Lady Caroline Lamb (1785–1828), as 'mad, bad and dangerous to know'.

Given Byron's ancestry it is perhaps unsurprising that he led the life he did. He was born in London on 22 January 1788 to Captain 'Mad' Jack Byron (1756–91), and his wife Catherine Gordon. His father's nickname was entirely justified. Mad Jack seems to have had only one interest in life – to spend as much money as possible in the shortest possible time. To escape these difficulties Byron's mother took him to Aberdeen when he was four. He attended Aberdeen Grammar School from 1794, and succeeded to the family title on the death of his great-uncle in 1798. He was sent to Harrow School in 1801 and went to Trinity College, Cambridge in 1805.

Verses and Vices

Byron published his first collection of verse, *Hours of Idleness*, under his own name in 1807. It was slated by Henry Brougham in the *Edinburgh Review*, but Byron sought his revenge by publishing *English Bards and Scotch Reviewers* (1809), a satire on poetry and its critics that described William Wordsworth as 'the meanest object of the lowly group'.

The row that followed his diatribe forced Byron to leave England in 1809. He travelled for two years and wrote the first and second parts of *Childe Harold's Pilgrimage*. The third part appeared in 1816 and the fourth in 1818. The poem made him famous – despite his earlier misbehaviour – and he was suddenly the most glamorous and sought-after man in London.

Fame seems to have gone to Byron's head and he began a series of affairs. He had a nine-month fling with Lady Caroline Lamb, whose husband was the future Prime Minister Viscount Melbourne. It is likely that he conducted other affairs simultaneously, but then came the bombshell – despite his love of the wild life, Byron had decided to marry.

The circumstances surrounding Byron's marriage and subsequent separation turned him from a demi-god into public enemy number one, and he was eventually forced to leave England for good – the fate it seems of many caught up in scandals in earlier times.

To general astonishment and against the advice of almost everyone, Byron married Annabella Milbanke (1792–1860) in 1815. She was a serious, devout and almost puritanical young lady. But after just a year, the marriage collapsed and Annabella returned to her parents, along with the couple's baby daughter, Augusta Ada. Any hope of reconciliation was non-existent and, as the details of their year together filtered out, Byron's name was blackened irredeemably. Evidence was gathered against him and Annabella was guarded round-the-clock, her parents fearful that Byron would attack their Leicestershire home.

But what had led to the sudden separation? And what were the rumours that have dogged Byron's legend ever since?

The main problem was simply one of huge incompatibility. It was widely speculated that Byron married Annabella to revenge himself on the respectable world she represented. Certainly, her parents heartily disliked him, which may explain the couple's short stay with them after their marriage. But the couple's troubles really began when they travelled to the splendidly named Six Mile Bottom in Suffolk to stay with Augusta, Byron's half-sister.

Years later, Annabella described some aspects of this period to the American writer Harriet Beecher Stowe. Annabella was immediately horrified at Byron's familiarity with his sister – in fact she was convinced that the relationship between the two was sexual. She watched the pair with horror until one evening Byron said to her: 'I suppose you perceive you are not wanted here. Go to your own room, and leave us alone. We can amuse ourselves better without you.' To add to the scandal of the siblings' relationship, it is likely that a daughter was born to the pair in 1814.

'The world will believe me'

It was at about this time that Byron also apparently told his young wife that he intended to sleep with whoever he liked and he advised her to do the same. She was aghast. By March 1816, the increasingly troubled couple were living at 13 Piccadilly Terrace in London – and Augusta was frequently with them. Byron was almost permanently drunk – a habit that deepened his natural melancholy and plunged him into moods of black despair. By all accounts he took out his rage on the hapless Annabella. She resolved to leave him and when she did, the egotistical poet completely misjudged the situation, commenting that 'the world will believe me, and it will not believe you'. However, despite his immense fame, the public sided with his young wife.

Annabella left Byron soon after the birth of their daughter on 10 December, 1815. She went to visit her parents in Leicestershire and never returned. Under her parents' guidance, she began an action to obtain a legal separation from her husband on the grounds of his incestuous relationship with his sister. Added to this, rumours of homosexuality, orgies and devil worship now surrounded the poet.

European Exile

Byron had no choice but to leave England again and this time it was for good. He took a boat to France on 25 April 1816, travelling with his friend Dr Polidori and others to Switzerland. The group stayed at the Villa Diodati on Lake Geneva, where soon another scandal-ridden poet, Percy Bysshe Shelley (1792–1822) turned up with his wife, Mary (1797–1851). It was while staying at the Villa Diodati that Mary Shelley began the most famous horror story in the English language – *Frankenstein, or the Modern Prometheus*.

Ever restless, Byron travelled to Greece in 1823 to join the revolution against the Turkish occupation. He died of a fever at Missolonghi on 19 April, 1824. His body was brought back to England and he was buried in the Byron family vault in the village church of Hucknall Torkard a few miles north of Nottingham. His daughter Ada was later buried beside him. When Byron's grave was opened in the 1920s his body was found to be remarkably well preserved.

One of the greatest scandals of Byron's life, however, was neither his relationship with his sister, nor his treatment of his wife. Rather, it was the destruction of his diaries. Byron had written the story of his life up to 1816 and he gave the manuscript to the poet Tom Moore. In a complicated arrangement, Moore then pledged the manuscript to the publisher John Murray for 2,000 guineas. When Byron died the two men read the manuscript and were so horrified – and terrified that someone else might read it – that they burned it in the fireplace at Murray's premises in Albemarle Street. The fireplace where this priceless manuscript was destroyed is still there. There is no doubt that Byron's diaries would have been the publishing sensation of that or any age.

> *'Man, being reasonable, must get drunk; The best of life is but intoxication'*
>
> Lord Byron

The Duke's Folly
Bentinck Scott, 5th Duke of Portland

Best known for building miles of passageways and a huge ballroom beneath the ground at Welbeck, his country house in Nottinghamshire, Bentinck Scott, the 5th Duke of Portland (1800–79) was so eccentric that even his family would not come near him and his behaviour was so unpredictable that people avoided him on the grounds that whatever bizarre 'disease' he had might be contagious.

Scott spent a fortune employing hard-up labourers on extraordinary building projects. He constructed everything from lakes and pagodas to a skating rink and a vast stable for his string of racehorses, none of which was ever entered for a race. He also built an underground railway between his house and his ballroom. The ballroom itself was over 170 feet long with a thousand soft gas lights – far more than was necessary to illuminate the room – and a ceiling painted to represent a sunset. Yet, in spite of all the expense, the ballroom was never used. The miles of tunnel, which ran right to the edge of the estate, were probably built so that he could move about his property without the risk of meeting anyone – making contact with people, whether informally or formally, was something he avoided at all costs.

Hidden From View

His dislike of seeing other people and being seen was so intense that Scott had a coach built with low seats and impenetrable blinds. This would be driven to the nearest railway station and loaded onto a carriage with the duke still in it; here he would remain right through the journey. One of the tunnels at Welbeck was big enough to accommodate a coach and four horses and the duke always entered his carriage in this tunnel so that he was not seen by anyone. His London home was similarly equipped in order to ensure his absolute privacy.

All those given a job on the estate were provided with a donkey and an umbrella. In the unlikely event Scott was seen by his employees, anyone who nodded, bowed, spoke or even glanced at him was instantly dismissed. It was the duke's one unfailing rule. The household staff were sent letters when the duke wanted to say something to them, and when he was ill he insisted on the doctor waiting outside his room while he shouted a description of his symptoms through the door. It is said that he had a vast collection of wigs, false beards and moustaches, which he wore when he went anywhere where there was the risk of being recognized.

When Scott inherited Welbeck, it had been a house full of treasures, including valuable pictures, furniture, books and tapestries. By the time he died virtually every room, including those underground, had been emptied and painted pink. Many were also found to contain a lavatory, carefully plumbed in, but fixed right in the middle of each room. After his death, the pictures he had bought and inherited – some of great value – were found stacked all over the place, but not one was hanging on a wall. It is believed that some time before he died he burned many pictures because he considered that they were not quite good enough for the house.

The Tichborne Affair
Roger Charles Tichborne

The Tichborne affair was one of the greatest – and most bizarre – scandals of the Victorian era. It lasted more than ten years, involved two of the longest and most expensive trials in legal history and pitted the aristocracy against the people.

Roger Charles Tichborne (1829–54) was heir to a vast fortune that had been amassed over generations by one of England's oldest and most prominent Catholic families. Tichborne spent his early years in France, where he learnt to speak fluent French. He returned to England when he was 16 and went to school at Stonyhurst, before becoming a soldier. When military life didn't work out Tichborne travelled to America and eventually to Brazil. He was lost at sea while sailing from Rio de Janeiro.

An Unlikely Claimant

However, Tichborne's mother, Henrietta Felicit, did not accept that her son was dead and she placed advertisements in newspapers all over the world in the belief that he had been washed up alive on some distant shore. In 1865, a butcher living in Wagga Wagga in Queensland, Australia, contacted her via an agency and claimed to be Roger.

While the real Tichborne had been tall and slim with black hair, the butcher was fat and fair with light-brown wavy hair. When he wrote to his supposed mother she must have noticed that he was virtually illiterate, but by then Henrietta was beyond all reason and obsessed with the idea that this individual was her son. When evidence appeared that he could not possibly be Roger, she simply ignored it, while pouncing on the least scrap that suggested he might be.

Almost as soon as the claimant came forward Henrietta sent him enough money to take a boat for England. On the way the butcher met a man who'd been a servant to a lord – it was later stated in court that the servant coached the claimant in the manners and behaviour of the aristocracy.

When he arrived in England the butcher visited Henrietta. While he was with her, something very odd happened – the family solicitor, for reasons that were never explained, accepted that he was indeed Roger Tichborne. So, too, did a local antiquary. Henrietta herself immediately declared herself satisfied that this man was her son despite the fact that he could not speak a word of French. The rest of the family was horrified.

The public was entranced by the story and fully supported the claimant. Henrietta gave him an allowance of £1,000 a year and passed her real son's diaries to him. Using these, he was able to play his role far more effectively.

Meanwhile, the rest of the Tichbornes, thoroughly rattled, employed investigators who discovered that the butcher's real name was Arthur Orton and that he originally came from Wapping. He'd deserted from a ship in Australia and taken the name Castro. They also discovered that when he arrived in London to claim his inheritance he'd visited his family in Wapping first.

Orton had been spending freely in expectation of his inheritance, and when his creditors pressed him for repayment the whole issue came to trial. After more than 100 days in court, Orton's claim to the Tichborne inheritance was rejected. In 1874, he was arrested for perjury. Another trial ensued at which Orton was found guilty and sentenced to 14 years.

People of all classes had supported Orton and continued to do so after his imprisonment. The situation became so serious that in 1875 the authorities in London were being warned that there might be a general insurrection in support of Orton. Attempts were made by his supporters to set up a Royal Commission to investigate the case, but they were resisted and the greatest cause célèbre of the age gradually subsided. When Orton was released from prison in 1884 he went on a lecture tour, but attendances were poor, and he was soon forgotten. He died in poverty in London in 1898.

The Woman on the Train
Valentine Baker

One of the greatest sexual scandals of the 19th century led to a complete change in the design of railway carriages. It also revealed the hypocrisy that allowed a gentleman to make sexual advances to his social inferiors but not under any circumstances to a 'gentlewoman'. Colonel Valentine Baker (1827–87) was a famous and respected soldier who had been given responsibility for organizing a grand review of the British Army in 1875. He made the mistake of compromising a young lady who, as the court put it, 'could not have been mistaken for a shop girl', as if such women were somehow a different species and therefore not worthy of the protection of the law.

The story began when Baker hopped on a train at the small station of Liphook, Hampshire. In those days, railway carriages consisted of a series of coaches bolted together in a row – there was no connecting passage, so once a passenger had entered a compartment they had to stay there until they got off. Baker entered a first-class compartment that was already occupied by a young woman named Kate Dickinson, who was heading to London en route for Switzerland.

He later admitted that he did start a conversation with the young woman. Fifty minutes into the journey, a workman spotted a young woman hanging out of the carriage door as the train hurtled through Woking. The alarm was raised and a red signal brought the train to a halt near Esher, where the woman was helped down on to the track. She told a guard that Baker had assaulted her and would not leave her alone.

Baker was locked into a compartment and not released until the train reached Waterloo. The next day, Dickinson's family issued a warrant for his arrest. The young woman claimed that Baker had 'insulted' her – the Victorian euphemism for sexual assault. By the time the case came to trial in 1875 the accusation was one of 'assault with attempt to ravish'. The newspapers were filled with gossip and innuendo about one of the juiciest cases of sexual misdemeanour in years. The case was made even more interesting because Baker held such a senior rank in the army and his brother was the famous explorer Sam Baker, who had also been involved in a scandal when he married a girl he'd bought in a Balkan slave market!

With Prejudice

With such extensive and biased press coverage, the jury was almost certainly prejudiced against Baker from the start. He protested his innocence. However, although we have no way of knowing exactly what he confided to his brother, some of his explanation must have been damning. Sam Baker wrote that 'Val must allow that even his best friends cannot defend even as much as he confesses'.

Baker was found guilty, imprisoned for a year and fined £500. He was cashiered by the Queen, which meant that he lost his job in the army. When he left prison he spent the remainder of his life fighting as an independent conscript in Turkey and the Near East in an attempt to redeem himself. As a direct result of the scandal surrounding the case, carriages on railway trains were modified and fitted with spy holes so that occupants could never be certain whether or not they were being watched.

Christie's Glyndebourne
John Christie

John Christie (1882–1962), who founded the Glyndebourne Festival of opera, was born into an aristocratic and somewhat eccentric land-owning family. By all accounts, he was an engaging yet extremely badly behaved child. At school he spent most of his time breaking windows, and was caned virtually every day for his misdemeanours. Apparently, Christie simply accepted this as part of everyday life.

At 13 he was sent to Eton, where he had the great good fortune, as he later described it, of coming under the influence of Dr Porter, an accomplished painter, musician and cyclist. Porter fostered a passion for the arts in the young Christie. After leaving Eton he embarked on an officer training course at Woolwich, but while there he had a serious riding accident that left him with a permanent limp. In 1902, he went up to Cambridge.

Already noted for his eccentric behaviour, Christie became fascinated by Richard Wagner (1813–83), hammering out the great composer's work on his piano in order to evoke the music's passion. He always played wearing a huge towel wrapped round his head, which he said he needed to catch the sweat from his exertions. He also played late into the night, much to the annoyance of his neighbours.

Eton's Eccentric

On coming down from Cambridge in 1906, Christie became a teacher at Eton, where he remained, to the delight of some boys and the horror of others (and their parents), for the next 16 years. He didn't need the small amount of money that teaching gave him, but it 'rather appealed', and he needed something to do. Students who remember being taught science by him describe his lessons as totally incomprehensible.

Contemporaries talked of Christie's prowess at cricket, a sport that he was particularly fond of. He was said to lumber towards the stumps when bowling, and at the last minute the ball would appear as if by magic from somewhere behind his head. He was described as terrifyingly violent on the football field, in spite of the fact that he always played in a pink silk vest.

By the time he reached his early 30s, his mother, Lady Rosamond, had become concerned that he had not married, so she began to send him pictures of eligible women that she had cut from the pages of *Tatler*. None quite took his fancy. Lady Rosamond also tried to persuade him to abandon teaching and take up life as a country squire at her house at Glyndebourne, Sussex. Christie resisted his mother and stayed at Eton until the First World War broke out in 1914. Despite the fact that he limped badly and had lost an eye in a sporting accident, he tricked medical officers into passing him fit for service.

His mother was sufficiently worried about him to use her influence to get him out of the Army, something that was considered quite acceptable for individuals from the upper classes to do at the time. In August 1916, Christie's first plans for the reconstruction of Glyndebourne were drawn up. He built an organ room and extra bedrooms and installed electricity.

After the war ended, Christie threw lavish weekend parties that scandalized the district. He spent hundreds of pounds on champagne, but refused to light fires or turn on the heating, however cold it became. When it grew dark, partygoers stumbled around, bumping into each other. In winter, Christie carried a small electric fire with him from room to room, simply plugging it in wherever he happened to decide to sit. He so hated to see fuel – particularly new-fangled electricity – wasted that he frequently turned the lights out when his guests were still sitting chatting, leaving them in the dark. Rumour had it that Christie took such measures to allow unseemly acts of vice to take place.

Christie continued to teach at Eton and, along with one or two other masters, he took up dancing. Pupils often saw him waltzing with a cushion as partner. Dining at Eton one winter evening, he proudly drew his neighbour's attention to the fact that, in spite of the cold, he was wearing a thin tropical suit and no vest. He was often seen boarding the London train with a large hot water bottle sticking out of the back of his trousers. When he got to Victoria he would unscrew it and tip the contents over the platform. In his car he always drove wrapped in a huge eiderdown and was occasionally stopped by suspicious policemen.

An Unconventional Aristocrat

In 1922, at the age of 40, he retired from Eton, and the amateur operatics that he had held during his weekend parties at Glyndebourne took on a new and more serious aspect. He had always insisted that his guests wear black tie to these events, although he always wore unconventional clothes – an enormous grubby suit and slippers or tennis shoes.

Though extremely rich, Christie was notoriously stingy. He travelled third class, he steamed off stamps that the post office had failed to mark, he refused to tip waiters, porters and bellboys, and he worried so much about wasting electricity that he eventually employed a man just to turn the lights off in his house. Female guests at Glyndebourne were always presented with knitting 'to keep them occupied'.

When he bought things, which he hated doing, he always bought in bulk. Thus when one of his secretaries needed a typewriter, he bought six; and he once had 2,000 pairs of plastic shoes made. He tried to sell them to a London store and, when that failed, thought about advertising them in the Glyndebourne Opera programme. Eventually, he littered his London club, Brook's, with them. He also delighted in going for a drive to get rid of his old clothes; he would whizz along the Bayswater Road hurling grubby collars and socks into the path of oncoming vehicles – 'it's much the easiest way to get rid of them', he would say. And, despite his personal concern for wasting electricity, if the electric light at his club or a friend's house was too bright, he would put up an umbrella rather than turn the light off.

The organ he built at Glyndebourne was so powerful that whenever it was played it brought parts of the roof crashing down, much to the terror of visitors. Eventually, Glyndebourne was expanded into a full opera house, as Christie had promised his wife, the opera singer Audrey Mildmay whom he married in 1931, that it would be. Within ten years it had become as famous as Covent Garden, but Christie's behaviour in his old age became increasingly bizarre. When he went bald he began regularly to sprinkle rum on his head; he insisted on performing in his own operas, even though he couldn't really sing, and after a visit to Austria he began to wear *lederhosen* and Tyrolean hats.

Horse Indoors
Lord Berners

He dyed his doves a dozen different colours, painted pictures of horses as they stood in his drawing room and had a harpsichord installed in the rear compartment of his Rolls Royce. Lord Berners (1883–1950) was one of the all-time great eccentrics and practical jokers. He is probably best remembered by some for the following couplet:

Red noses last a lifetime
Red roses but a day.

With a large residence, Faringdon House in Oxfordshire, and a private income, Berners could behave as madly as he pleased without worrying about offending people. He erected a tall tower on his grounds, and then put up a sign at its foot that stated 'Members of the public who commit suicide from this tower do so at their own risk'. Another sign on the estate declared 'dogs will be shot, cats will be whipped'. He loved having horses in the house, and once invited Penelope Chetwode, who was married to the poet John Betjeman, *and* her horse to a tea party.

> *'Members of the public who commit suicide from this tower do so at their own risk'*
>
> Lord Berners

A Man Not to Annoy

Berners was a generous host and a loyal friend, but those he took a dislike to – and there were many – often ended up the butt of a practical joke. For example, when a diplomat once annoyed him, he tied his spectacles to an open ink bottle

ABOVE: *Sir Gerald Hugh Tyrwhitt-Wilson, 14th Baron Berners, composer and painter, on his chaise longue at Faringdon House in Oxfordshire.*

and a collection of pens and paper clips, so that when the diplomat rose to make an important speech and reached for his glasses, the whole lot was dragged onto his lap.

Berners hated sharing a carriage if he travelled by train, so to avoid this he wore a black skull cap on rail journeys. If there were a risk that others might get on and join him in his carriage as the train approached a station, Berners would lean out of the window and solemnly invite them in. Of course they were so terrified by this bizarre apparition that he was left alone.

Berners' highly unconventional behaviour caused scandal among his neighbours. Years after his death, local villagers in Oxfordshire still talked about the outrageous goings-on at the estate – wild parties, men dressed up as women, horses cavorting up and down the stairs and, in the midst of it all, Lord Berners doing as he pleased regardless of the chaos around him.

La Vice Anglaise
English Pleasures

The French are convinced – and always have been – that the true Englishman only really enjoys one kind of sexual activity. Known in French as *La Vice Anglaise*, it has its origins in public-school punishments involving the cane. Having been soundly beaten on the buttocks for so many of their formative years, many public schoolboys find that in adulthood they miss the regular swish of the cane and the resulting tingle on the posterior.

Of course, this really only applies to older public-school educated men as flagellation – or corporal punishment – is now largely a thing of the past. But, for those over 50, the cane has echoes of their golden youth when bigger, more handsome boys could be relied on to chastize their recalcitrant juniors. As a result of this unusual sexual proclivity, brothels sprang up all over England to cater for the taste – particularly in the Victorian period when schoolboys were whipped for almost everything.

A Bit of What You Fancy

Politicians, senior figures in the church, lords, great painters and writers – half the population of London's eminent clubs appear to have frequented houses where they could be sure of a severe if discreet beating. Having enjoyed

LEFT: THE ILLUSTRATOR AUBREY BEARDSLEY, WHO WAS ACCUSED OF SLEEPING WITH HIS HALF-SISTER, REGULARLY DREW SCENES INVOLVING FLAGELLATION.

this they then went home to their wives. One of the most interesting examples of aristocratic masochism involved the artist Francis Bacon (see pages 80–81) who was regularly thrashed as a child and developed a taste for it that never left him.

La Vice Anglaise has many sub-divisions – and brothels offering all kinds of related humiliations are still popular wherever respectable gentlemen are to be found. There are brothels where men dress up as babies (even wearing nappies) while prostitutes wander around breastfeeding them and occasionally telling them off for soiling themselves. The most curious aspect of sexual pleasure gained from being beaten or humiliated is that it appeals mostly to men in positions of power and authority, which may make many of us look at our bosses in a completely new light! Yes, the English public-school system certainly has a lot to answer for when it comes to deeply suspicious sexual behaviour!

Beyond the Pale –
Infamous Eccentrics and Academics

'I am not over-fond of
resisting temptation.'
William Beckford

Britain's Meanest Men
John Elwes and Daniel Dancer

In early 18th-century London there were two men who became a byword for avarice, greed and meanness. John Elwes (c. 1730–89) and Daniel Dancer (1716–94) were said to have brought shame on humanity with their appalling behaviour.

Southwark's Miser

Elwes was born into a family of notorious misers that had made its money from brewing and had lived in Southwark for generations. His mother is said to have died from malnutrition, in spite of having tens of thousands of pounds in the bank, and although John was apparently an exceptionally bright child, he rarely opened a book after leaving school. In fact, as his desire to make money grew he gave up everything else, including riding, which had been a passion in his youth.

In his twenties, John began to visit his uncle, Sir Harvey Elwes. He always changed into rags before he reached the house, so terrified was he that his uncle, a notorious skinflint, would take offence at his decent clothes and disinherit him. Uncle and nephew would sit in the dark by a fire made with one stick, sharing a glass of wine until bedtime. They would then creep upstairs, still in the dark, to save the cost of a candle.

When he came into his inheritance, Elwes became fanatically stingy. He walked from one end of London to the other in the heaviest rain rather than part with sixpence for a coach; he ate maggot-infested meat; he never lit a fire to dry his

LEFT: *JOHN ELWES WOULD RATHER EAT MAGGOTS THAN SPEND HIS FORTUNE.*

clothes; he wore a wig that had been thrown into a ditch by a beggar and a coat that had gone green with age – it had belonged to a long-dead ancestor and had been found blocking a hole in the wall of the house. When he rode to London – he was an MP for more than ten years – he always carried an egg or two in his pocket and slept in a hedge rather than pay the cost of lodgings and he always rode his horse on the grass verge instead of on the road for fear that its shoes would wear out too quickly.

Elwes owned houses all over London, as well as an estate in Suffolk, but took a few pieces of furniture with him each time he travelled, rather than furnish each residence. He died at the age of 59 and left more than three-quarters of a million pounds – an immense sum for the day – to his two sons.

Harrow's Penny-pinching Residents

Daniel Dancer was born in Harrow Weald in Middlesex where his father owned a considerable amount of property and land. Little is recorded of his earliest years, but by his early 20s he shared the family house with his sister who, on the rare occasions that she ventured out, was usually dressed in layers of rags – 'a mixture of male and female attire tied round with a ravelling of hemp' – and armed with a broomstick or pitchfork to attack anyone who ventured onto her brother's property.

Their house was patched, boarded and repaired to an extraordinary degree, and hardly a stick of furniture remained in one piece because Dancer used wood from it to carry out repairs. Not only did he have to keep out the weather, he also had to plug holes to keep out the hordes of cats attracted by the huge numbers of vermin that roamed the house. Thrift was carried to absurd lengths. For example, a neighbour called one day and found him pulling the nails out of a pair of bellows. He needed the nails, he said, to fix a piece of leather over a hole in the wall and he thought the bellows could spare the nails and save him the expense of buying any. 'Undertakers, trunk-makers and bellows-makers are the most extravagant fellows in the world in their profusion of nails,' he said.

Each Saturday, Dancer bought a three-pound piece of the cheapest cut of beef and boiled it with a dozen or so hard dumplings. This had to sustain both Dancer and his sister until the following Saturday. Occasionally, their diet was supplemented by the bones that Dancer came across during his long walks – yet for all this he had an annual income of £3,000, at a time when a labourer was expected to be able to keep a family of six on £30 a year.

One summer morning, Dancer took his usual walk across Harrow Common, looking for bones, sticks, rags and anything else that might be useful to eat or to repair the house with, when he came across a dead sheep. The sheep had clearly been deceased for some time, but for Dancer this was a rare prize and he dragged it home in triumph. He and his sister lived on the beast for weeks – they boiled it, roasted it and made it into pies. When they were down to the last few dozen pies, Dancer locked them away in a chest because he felt they were being eaten too quickly.

In spite of half-starving himself continually, Dancer was hugely sentimental about animals, and his dog was always fed on the best meat and milk. He kept a horse, too, but to save money, he had only its front two feet shod. He walked into London once to invest £2,000, and while waiting outside an office in the city he was mistaken for a beggar and given a penny. He told the story to anyone who would listen for the rest of his life.

Look After the Pennies...

A neighbour named Lady Tempest eventually persuaded Dancer to buy a hat to protect himself against the weather, although he insisted on buying a second-hand one. He wore it for some time, and then Lady Tempest noticed that he was not wearing it. She asked what had happened, and Dancer told her with great pleasure that he'd sold the hat for sixpence more than he'd paid for it.

During his last few years, it was said that Dancer slept in a sack with a hay beehive on his head. His favourite occupation night and day, but mostly at night when he couldn't be seen by anyone else, was to visit the hundred and one holes and corners about the house and barns where he had hidden gold, notes and silver coins. Yet when the house was burgled, robbers could find absolutely nothing.

When he died at the age of 78, Dancer's heirs found £2,500 hidden in a dung-heap. In an old jacket nailed to the stable door they found £500 in gold and notes, and there were banknotes in every cushion and bolster, in the sofa, in milk jugs and in bowls. In more than 20 holes in the chimney £200 was found in soot-blackened notes. In an old cracked teapot £600 was found, and on a small slip of paper left lying on top of the notes was a scrap of paper on which Dancer had written 'not to be too hastily overlooked'.

The Academic In A Glass Case
Jeremy Bentham

The philosopher Jeremy Bentham (1748–1832) was one of the great political and social thinkers of the late 18th and early 19th centuries. He published more than 60 works that covered subjects as diverse as the need for political

OPPOSITE: *JEREMY BENTHAM LIKED TO MAKE A DISPLAY OF HIMSELF.*

reform, animal welfare, the state of the colonies and the evils of swearing. Most famously, he is associated with the idea of utilitarianism – a doctrine that believed in the greatest good for the greatest number. Bentham was considered a walking scandal in his day, however, for advocating universal suffrage and the decriminalization of homosexuality.

Bentham was also closely involved in the idea of a dissenter's university. Dissenters – those who refused to conform to the beliefs of the Church of England – were not allowed to study at the traditional universities so they set up their own. The University of London, which began life as an establishment for dissenters, was founded in 1828 when Bentham was in his 80s. Although he took no practical part in establishing the institution, he is often considered to be its spiritual father, largely because of his advocacy of religious tolerance and education for all.

Bentham loved the new university, so it should come as no surprise that he left University College all his manuscripts. But he also left a legacy of surpassing eccentricity. Visitors to the South Cloisters of the main building cannot fail to see a large wooden and glass cabinet that stands in the corridor.

The Preserved Philosopher

Inside the cabinet is a surprisingly life-like and life-sized Jeremy Bentham, comfortably seated with a stick in his hand and dressed in the very clothes he wore in life. The figure is not a model – it is actually the preserved corpse of the great man. When it was first placed here following his death in 1832, the head and face were actually Bentham's own; however, the embalming technique used wasn't up to scratch, and the head deteriorated so badly that a wax replica was made. Bentham had left his body to the college on condition that it was preserved in this way and one imagines his skeleton keeps an eye on the academic world he so loved in life.

Legends about the preserved philosopher abound – one says that he is wheeled into every university council meeting. At the end of each meeting the minutes record that he is 'present but not voting'. Another legend states that for a decade before he died Bentham carried around the glass eyes he wanted used in his preserved head. When they were finally installed, they fell out and the head itself fell off and was found between Bentham's feet.

No one knows why Bentham stipulated that he should be preserved and set up for public display in this way, but it ties in well with the philosophy of a man who took a practical view of affairs and who thought it was important to make a contribution to the day-to-day life of the society in which he lived. At the end of his life he probably thought it would be nice to be in a position where he could watch some important part of the world go by. The cabinet in the cloisters is probably as good a place as any.

A Towering Gothic Genius
William Beckford

William Beckford (1760–1844) was born into one of the richest families in Britain; however, the Beckfords were also fierce, arrogant, eccentric and occasionally violent. Despite such a pedigree, William was to prove the most infamous Beckford of them all.

William was born at the vast and beautiful Fonthill Manor, which he later had pulled down. Nicknamed 'Splendens' by the locals, the Palladian house was opulent in the extreme – the ceilings were painted by some of the foremost Italian painters of the day and every room was filled with fabulous ornate furniture and statuary. One vast room, the Turkish Room, was flamboyantly oriental in style with arabesques covering the ceiling and looking-glass windows to increase the sense of space.

The young William had a short temper, but he also had an uncharacteristically gentle side. In later life he was famous for his unpredictability – one minute he would beat his servants, the next give them large sums of money. By the time he was 60, William had spent the family fortune, mostly trying to build the tallest structure the world had ever seen – Fonthill Abbey in Wiltshire was a vast gothic complex of turrets and towers, passages and spiral staircases, secret doors, tunnels and dungeons.

In 1777, Beckford visited Geneva where he learned Italian, Spanish, German and Portuguese with extraordinary rapidity. It was a trip that changed him from the hunting, drinking squire his father approved of into an artistic individual. He was so taken by the cultured environment of Geneva that on his return to England, he refused to hunt, shoot or fish, and for the rest of his life he referred to anglers and butterfly hunters as torturers.

His mother, who he called the Begum, tried repeatedly to turn him away from the artistic pursuits he favoured and push him towards more traditional country pursuits. But Beckford would have none of it. Before long, a scandal involving the son of a family friend, with whom Beckford is thought to have had a sexual relationship, led to disaster. So great was the controversy that any chance he had of being accepted as part of society ended forever. Instead William was packed off to the Continent for the Grand Tour, narrowly escaping prosecution for immorality.

An Oriental Romance

By 1782, Beckford had started writing the oriental romance that was to make him famous. *Vathek* was a tale in which evil appeared to triumph, only to be rewarded with eternal damnation in the end. First published in French, the book was printed in English in 1786. It was an immensely popular and influential novel, inspiring work by Samuel Johnson and later Benjamin Disraeli. However, the publication of *Dreams, Waking Thoughts* in 1783 led to more trouble for Beckford, primarily because the work mocked the Church and the traditional pursuits of the English landed gentry. As a result, the Establishment resolved to have nothing whatever to do with him. After a further sexual scandal – no proof of which was ever offered – Beckford was ostracized by virtually everyone. He was continually snubbed and ignored for the remaining 60 years of his life.

He retired briefly to Splendens, and then set out for Portugal where he was to spend a year and a half with a deeply religious aristocratic family. He then went to Spain where, ever inclined to get himself into trouble, he fell in love with the French ambassador's 18-year-old daughter, her 14-year-old husband and his brother! By 1788, Beckford was forced to flee to Paris, but a year later he had returned discreetly to Fonthill, where he began landscaping the gardens on a huge scale.

A Monumental Construction

It was the beginning of an astonishing building spree that was to consume the family fortune. Beckford employed the celebrated architect James Wyatt (1746–1813), with whom he argued constantly, and began work on a vast gothic abbey. Hundreds of workmen were engaged, and vastly overpaid because Beckford, uninterested in the practical details of building, thought money would be the decisive factor in getting the project completed as quickly as possible.

By 1797, Fonthill's first great tower was completed. A few weeks later it blew down during a storm, probably because Beckford had continually goaded and bribed Wyatt and his men into working faster and faster. Beckford shrugged off this disaster, however, and building started all over again.

In 1800, to the surprise of almost everyone, Lord Nelson visited the house and Beckford organized a huge reception for him. But, in spite of Nelson's visit, Beckford remained a social outcast, perhaps because the two men found they didn't like each other anyway. Nelson upset Beckford by complaining he'd been driven too fast in Beckford's carriage, and Beckford upset Nelson by trying to buy a peerage.

Using threats and more threats, Beckford managed to get his abbey, complete with its 276-foot tower, finished by 1807. The tallest building in Europe, Fonthill was the physical embodiment of a dream, designed to shock and amaze – and it did. It also led the way to some of the greatest gothic building of the early 19th century, including the Houses of Parliament.

Fonthill had two turrets that reached over 100 feet high, as well as a spectacular octagonal tower that was influenced by Ely Cathedral. From north to south the building measured 312 feet and 270 feet from east to west. But what looked so imposing and magnificent from the outside was actually rotten through and through. Beckford had pushed his builders and architects to such an extent that the workmanship was of the poorest quality.

Boredom and Bankruptcy

Having built Fonthill, Beckford almost immediately lost interest in it. He was bored with his life, which he spent riding endlessly around the estate allowing no one in. It was even rumoured that he occasionally threw himself from his horse into the lake to relieve his boredom.

BELOW: *As a young man, William Beckford was packed off to the Continent in order to avoid any further embarrassment for his family.*

For much of his adult life, William was accompanied by an unattractive dwarf from Switzerland, who ate only mushrooms; an obscure Italian called Franchi, who seemed half-confidante and half-servant; and several monkeys and dogs. Beckford himself was a tall, slim man with regular features, apart from a rather long nose that gave him a permanent look of disdain.

By 1822, Beckford had spent his entire fortune and bankruptcy threatened. Fonthill was leaky and uncomfortable and, as impetuous as ever, Beckford decided to sell the lot. More than 70,000 copies of the Christie's catalogue produced for the sale were bought, and people came from all over the country to view the astonishing treasure trove of furniture, books, pictures and other valuable objects. However, Beckford changed his mind at the last minute and sold the house and its contents to a Mr Farquhar. He was finally able to pay off his huge debts, and he apparently left Fonthill without so much as a backward glance.

In December of the same year, the high tower at Fonthill collapsed, destroying most of the rest of the house. It was only by a miracle that no one was injured. Farquhar made the best of it and rejoiced in the fact that he now had a smaller, more manageable house in which to live. Beckford expressed neither interest nor concern. The smaller Lancaster Tower, the Oratory and the Sanctuary are all that now remain of one of the most eccentric houses ever built in Britain.

The Buckland Menagerie
William and Frank Buckland

William Buckland (1784–1856) was Dean of Westminster and a fanatical collector of animals. His house in London was crammed with thousands of natural history specimens – some were dead and some alive; some he slept with and others he ate. Guests at Buckland's house were likely to be offered roast hedgehog or a slice of grilled crocodile steak – and if they partook, the chances were that the meal came from an animal that had once roamed Buckland's house and garden as a pet! Buckland's friends tried to curb his insane passion, but nothing could be done and his behaviour became ever more notorious.

On one occasion, to prove the efficacy of bird droppings as fertilizer, Buckland scandalized his Oxford college by using great quantities of it to write the word 'guano' on their lawn. When the summer came and the grass had grown the letters could be clearly seen.

The King's Heart

William's friend Edward Harcourt, Archbishop of York (1757–1847), was, like Buckland himself, a great collector of curiosities and had managed to obtain what he believed to be the shrunken, mummified heart of Louis XIV. He kept it in a snuffbox in his London house and rashly showed it to William. 'I have eaten many things,' William is reported to have said, 'but never the heart of a king.' He then popped it into his mouth and swallowed it whole. Harcourt never forgave him.

Like Father, Like Son

Frank Buckland (1826–80), William's son, was even more outrageous than his father. He, too, was a naturalist and collector of animals of every description. Throughout his life, Frank dined regularly on rhinoceros, elephant and giraffe as he had friends at London Zoo who contacted him when any interesting animal died. He also swapped eels and trout for the body parts of patients who had died in the local hospital – not to eat, but for experiments in disection or mummification.

After leaving Oxford, Buckland decided to become a surgeon in London, but first, like most young men of his background at the time, he left for an extended period of study abroad – encouraged by family members who had heard the gossip about their increasingly odd relative. At a garden party after his return to London, Buckland turned up with his pet bear, Tig, in tow. He had dressed the creature in a scholar's cap and gown and proceeded to introduce it to the assembled glitterati, which included Florence Nightingale, several princes and the nephew of Napoleon. Not surprisingly, the guests were terrified. Tig eventually ended up in London Zoo after being caught trying to rob a sweet shop.

Once, as Buckland was buying a railway ticket at King's Cross, his pet monkey, Jacko, popped its head out of a bag. The stationmaster insisted that the monkey would have to be paid for, too. After a long and fruitless argument, an extremely exasperated Buckland pulled his pet tortoise out of a pocket and asked what fare he would have to pay for that. 'No charge for them, Sir, them be insects,' came the stationmaster's reply.

In spite of the fact that his house was already filled with animals, both dead and alive, Buckland continued to trawl London's docks in search of specimens; although he was adding continually to his collection, he never threw anything away.

In 1850, to the horror of his family, he married Hannah Papps, a coachman's daughter. Luckily for Buckland, she seemed to enjoy his mania for collecting animals as much as he did – at least there is no evidence that she objected to the hordes of monkeys one visitor saw sitting round the Buckland fireplace. 'They did terrible damage and bit everyone, but he loved them dearly,' he commented. But rats could also be seen running everywhere, over desks and tables and around the mongoose and donkey that also had the run of the place.

When his animals grew old or died Buckland often ate them, although he abhorred cruelty. He had consumed many things in his time, and pronounced mole to be 'poo' and bluebottle 'worse'.

The Eccentric Fisheries Inspector

Buckland was appointed Her Majesty's Inspector of Fisheries, and in this capacity was responsible for making sure that migratory fish were able to travel up Britain's rivers. While helping to construct a salmon ladder on the Thames, he put up a sign for the benefit of any fish stuck in the weir below the then unbuilt ladder. 'No road at present over the weir,' it read, 'go down-stream, take the first turning to the right and you will find good travelling water upstream and no jumping required.'

Often Buckland had so many specimens in various stages of decomposition that his whole house stank, but he never seemed to notice, probably because he was intrigued by the processes of decay. He took little care of his own health, always travelling without a hat or a coat, however cold the weather. He died at the age of 54, and wrote in his will 'God is so good, so very good to the little fishes that I do not believe he would let their inspector suffer shipwreck.'

The Maddest Squire in England
John Mytton

John Mytton (1796–1834) was surely one of the most badly behaved men who ever lived. He was the most famous – or infamous – member of a prominent Shropshire family that descended from a Norman nobleman called Reginald de Mutton. He was expelled from three distinguished public schools – Eton, Westminster and Harrow – something that is probably a record in itself. The reason for these expulsions was 'scandalous ignoble behaviour unfitting in a gentleman'. He was then taught privately, but his tutor didn't last long, as Mytton attacked him, knocking him about so badly that he refused to have anything to do with him again.

Mytton agreed to attend Oxford on the condition that he would never have to open a book, and, in the finest tradition of accepting wealthy students on their own terms, the university agreed. But even this was no good and Mytton quickly dropped out. Cambridge couldn't hold him either. At the age of 18 he set off on a grand tour of Europe. On his return to England, he began a life of madness that was to cost him one of the largest fortunes in England.

Mytton could be savage one minute and generous the next, as an incident in 1826 proved. He was out hunting when his hounds were distracted by someone shouting. He discovered a very large, very angry Welsh miner who was trying to turn Mytton's hounds onto another hare. Furious, Mytton immediately challenged the man to a boxing match. Despite being twice the size of his opponent, the miner gave up after 20 bare-knuckle rounds with Mytton, who made up in determination what he lacked in skill. Having beaten the miner, Mytton immediately gave him ten shillings to drink to his health. Such behaviour was quite typical of the man.

Dicing with Death

Mytton always wore thin silk stockings and shoes so that his feet became soaked as soon as it rained. He didn't wear a coat, whatever the weather, and his waistcoat and shirt were as often as not left undone. In the deepest snow or hardest frost he stomped through thick undergrowth or waded through lakes and ditches as if it were summer. He once lay half-naked for hours in the snow hoping to shoot a goose; and on another occasion he went duck shooting in the middle of the night in his nightshirt. His well-born neighbours never forgave him for these semi-naked adventures.

For most of his schooldays and throughout the rest of his life he is said to have drunk between five and eight bottles of port a day – and in those days port was twice as strong as it is now. If the port ran out Mytton drank scent,

BELOW: *JOHN MYTTON ONCE TRIED SETTING FIRE TO HIMSELF.*

lavender water or eau-de-cologne – he claimed the latter was excellent protection against the night air.

Although he only lived to be 38 years old, his acquaintances thought it was little short of a miracle that he lived so long, as it was said that he deliberately diced with death every day. He couldn't swim, but he would frequently throw himself into deep water, and he liked nothing better than for his horse or his carriage to run away with him – particularly if there was a good chance that the horse would fall and break its neck or that the carriage would overturn.

In one of his most infamous escapades he was driving a gig with a friend seated beside him. The friend expressed a 'strong regard for his neck', whereupon Mytton asked – caution being an automatic irritant – 'Were you ever much hurt, then, by being upset in a gig?' 'No, thank God,' said his friend. 'What,' cried Mytton. 'Never upset in a gig? Well, a damned slow fellow you must have been all your life!' And running his near wheel up a bank, he deliberately tipped them all over.

One day, finding himself bored in Shrewsbury, Mytton released two live foxes in the bar of the Lion Inn. In the chaos that followed most of the furniture and crockery was smashed.

Money Madness

Mytton had a cavalier attitude to money. On one occasion he borrowed £10,000 and immediately gave £9,000 of it to a friend who promptly disappeared, never to be seen again. Mytton was apparently unperturbed.

As he grew older, instead of calming down, or at least moderating his mad pranks, he seemed to grow wilder and more reckless. One night two men dined with him and won money off him at cards. Mytton saw them to their horses, but then ran to the back of the house, dressed up as a highwayman and galloped through the woods, where he cut off the two men a few miles from the park. He then held them up in time-honoured fashion and made them give up all the money they were carrying.

When things got very bad financially a solicitor told him that he could rescue his debts and avoid selling the family home if he agreed to live on £6,000 a year – a fortune by today's standards. Mytton's response was typical – 'I would not give a damn to live on £6,000 a year'. In fact, he spent a total of £500,000 in 15 years.

As his money ran out he took to walking everywhere, always sending his coach ahead even in the heaviest downpour. Eventually, the list of his unpaid bills grew so enormous that he was imprisoned, first in Shrewsbury and then in London, where he refused all offers of help. Released at last, he was later obliged to escape to France to avoid his creditors for the second time. He died on 29 March 1834.

The Most Wicked Man in the World
Aleister Crowley

If background is anything to go by, Aleister Crowley (1875–1947) should never have become a scandalous misfit, but by the time he died he was known as 'the most wicked man in the world'. It was an unlikely role for a man born into a family of Plymouth Brethren, a sect so devoted to the teachings of the Bible that even today they refuse to watch television or use computers. However, Crowley decided that there was more to life than praying for two or three hours a day.

Even as a young child he managed to alienate his devout parents – his mother called him 'the Beast 666', which delighted Crowley who kept the name for the rest of his life. By the age of 14 he was already sexually promiscuous, something that continued at Cambridge University. Here he was introduced to some newly fashionable books, including *The Kabbalah Unveiled* and works on magic by A.E. Waite.

> '*Do what thou wilt shall be the whole of the law.*'
>
> *Aleister Crowley*

Inspired, Crowley joined a bizarre group called the Hermetic Order of the Golden Dawn, becoming a full member in 1898 and moving to Scotland where he rented a house on the shores of Loch Ness. He tried to take over the Hermetic Order, but his coup was defeated by older members and he set off for Paris with another disgruntled member – MacGregor Nathers, who had translated *The Kabbalah Unveiled*. Together they cooked up a plan to break into the London premises of the Golden Dawn and change all the locks! They did so, and the other members took them to court.

By 1900, Crowley's sexual activities, which included sleeping with underage girls, had reached the ears of the authorities and rather than risk prosecution he went to Mexico. Two years later he was back in England where he married. His wife, Rose Kelly, was able to go into trances and claimed she could contact ancient Egyptian spirits. Crowley seems to have believed every mumbled word and he made her ramblings the basis of his book *Liber al vel Legis* or *The Book of the Law*. The basic message of the work was to do whatever one pleased, which was precisely what Crowley had always done anyway.

Sex, Drugs and Demons

Crowley travelled to India where he deserted his wife and child, returned to England and set up a branch of an organization devoted to 'sex magic'. This was the 'Ordo Templi Orientis'. Crowley claimed that he encountered the demon Chronozon through the sect. Throughout these years he had a string of mistresses on whom he would practise his sex magic, but by the 1920s he was hopelessly in debt and seriously addicted to heroin.

A legacy enabled him to set up the Abbey of Thelema at a remote farmhouse in Italy. Here he entertained his friends – or at least those who wanted to enjoy his drug-taking orgies. There were many takers. By this time Crowley had become a byword for debauchery and sin – in fact his behaviour was considered so appalling that serious commentators really believed he was either the devil or his right-hand man. Crowley wrote a number of books, including *Diary of a Drug Fiend*, and even today there are those who believe that he really was a magician and not just a deluded man devoted to sex and drugs. With his debts piling up Crowley eventually retired to Hastings where he died.

A Scandalous Scientist
John Burdon Sanderson Haldane

Born into a fiercely academic family, John Burdon Sanderson Haldane (1892–1964) spent much of his childhood lying in the meadows around Oxford with corn stuffed up the legs of his trousers in the hope that local pigeons would land and forage around his thighs. This was at the beginning of a life devoted to science and scandal.

In 1904, Haldane was sent to Eton where he was once beaten every day for a whole week. However, he was already showing signs of brilliance at science and mathematics, which led to his distinguished – and occasionally outrageous – career.

With the outbreak of war in 1914, Haldane, along with many of his student colleagues, left New College, Oxford and enlisted. Earl Haig is reputed to have described him as 'the bravest and dirtiest soldier in my army'. Injured by the blast from a massive shell he awoke to find himself being driven toward a field hospital by the future King Edward VIII. Many thought that Haldane's experiences in the trenches had left him relatively unscathed, but he always maintained that nothing after the war seemed real. He once wrote that he believed that his life after 1918 had all been entirely imaginary. 'Perhaps I will eventually wake up,' he mused.

Chemical Cocktails

Back at New College, Haldane resumed his academic studies and began teaching. He made himself ill by consuming large quantities of dangerous chemicals as part of experiments that he refused to carry out on animals. On one occasion he drank so much hydrochloric acid that he rode home on his bicycle feeling, as he said himself, 'like a demented devil'. On another occasion he was discovered running furiously up and down a long staircase to test the effects of almost two ounces of bicarbonate of soda that he'd swallowed.

Blithely unaware of the fact that other people did not always take kindly to the idea of being experimented on, Haldane once caused a stampede at a scientific symposium in Scotland by making pepper gas to demonstrate the kind of thing soldiers had to put up with in the trenches. People ran from the hall clutching their throats, their eyes streaming. The lecture was abandoned.

A Willing Adulterer

After years at Oxford, Haldane moved to Cambridge in 1922 where he decided to get married, although there was a slight hitch because his bride-to-be was already wed. However, this was no obstacle for Haldane. First he went to see the vice-chancellor of the university and announced that he was about to commit adultery. Knowing that for the divorce to go through his lover's husband would need proof of wrongdoing, Haldane enlisted the help of the private detective who had already been hired by his rival! He told him precisely which hotel the adulterous act would be committed in and even gave him the room number. Haldane was caught, just as he'd planned, and the story appeared in the newspapers. There was a huge scandal – but his lover got her divorce. However, the adverse publicity surrounding the case meant that Haldane lost his readership at Cambridge – he was furious.

Haldane settled into married life. He was devoted to animals and spent months training his cat to sit on top of the door into his sitting room and attack anyone who came in. He even adored the spiders that eventually infested his house as he refused to remove their webs. He loved to quote the disciple of Rousseau who, when asked by a lawyer to crush a spider, replied: 'If some superior being should say to a companion, "kill that lawyer" how should you like it? And a lawyer is more noxious to most people than a spider.' In 1932, Haldane left Cambridge for London, still smarting over his treatment by the authorities following his adultery.

Chemical Reaction

In 1945, he divorced his first wife and married his research assistant. By this time his temper had become notorious in academic circles; it had worsened considerably, probably as a result of the large quantities of chemicals he continually consumed for his experiments. He insulted everyone who came near him. When the BBC asked if they could film a discussion between Haldane and three other eminent scientists, they secretly agreed to film the men separately because they thought Haldane might attack one of the others.

Increasingly fed up with London, he moved to India in 1957 – although the official reason he gave was that after 60 years he was fed up wearing socks! In India he spent a great deal of his time helping injured animals.

Haldane was diagnosed as having cancer in 1964, but wasn't in the least offended when the BBC asked if they could film him for his own obituary. During the filming there was a close-up of him doodling – what the BBC crew didn't realize was that he was scribbling obscenities in Greek! Undaunted by his illness and as brave as he had been half-a-century earlier in the trenches, he wrote a long comic poem called 'Cancer's a Funny Thing'. When he died he left his body to science.

Wintle's Whimsies
Lieutenant-Colonel Alfred Wintle

Lieutenant-Colonel Alfred Daniel Wintle (1897–1966) was born in Russia where his father was employed as a diplomat. In spite of his Russian birth – or perhaps because of it – Wintle claimed that he got down on his knees every night before he went to bed and thanked God for making him an Englishman. To be an Englishman was, he said, 'the highest responsibility as well as the greatest honour'.

The gift of an umbrella when he was 12 made him feel he was 'on the way to becoming a complete English gentleman – it was the apple of my eye'. In fact he was so fond of this umbrella that he slept with it and placed a rolled-up note in it that said 'This umbrella has been stolen from A.D. Wintle'.

Man of Action

As soon as the First World War started Wintle joined up. On his first day in the trenches the soldier standing next to him was killed. Initially paralyzed with terror, Wintle then saluted the dead man. 'That did the trick,' he later said '… within 30 seconds I had again become an English man of action.' A few months later he narrowly missed being killed himself when a shell blew him off his horse. He lost his left eye and most of his left hand, but he was apparently more concerned about the welfare of his horse and relieved to hear that it was unharmed.

When the Armistice was signed in 1918 he noted in his diary: 'I declare private war on Germany'. From that day on he claimed that the Germans were merely lying low, and that the First and Second World Wars were actually two parts of the same conflict – something that many historians later agreed with. However, Wintle's belief that the war wasn't truly over led to a period

ABOVE: *Alfred Wintle thanked God for making him an Englishman.*

of apparently insane behaviour that eventually landed him in the Tower of London. As part of his campaign to convince officialdom that the conflict hadn't ended, he lobbied Whitehall officials continually until they could stand it no more and he was posted to Ireland.

By 1938, Wintle was back in England working in military intelligence, but he couldn't remain silent in the face of what he saw as the incompetence of his superiors. With the outbreak of the Second World War in 1939, Wintle made strenuous efforts to see active service, even though he was well into middle age. He went to see his MP and presented himself at medical boards disguising the fact that he had only one eye; but it was to no avail. He then attempted to get to France by impersonating a senior officer and trying to steal an aeroplane. This led to a much-publicized court martial when Commodore Boyle, the man Wintle had impersonated, decided to prosecute. Before the trial date was set, however, Wintle visited Boyle, threatened him with a loaded revolver, and told him that he ought to be shot for doing so little. The next morning Wintle was arrested and taken to the Tower of London.

By now the authorities were thoroughly embarrassed by the whole affair, which was on the front-page of every newspaper in the land. In an attempt to dampen the situation, they offered Wintle a way out. But to their horror he insisted on a trial, as he thought it would be great fun. He was found guilty of assault and given a severe reprimand. Back in the saddle, he went to North Africa and then, because he spoke fluent French and German, he was sent to work undercover in Nazi-occupied France.

Wintle vs Nye

At the end of the war Wintle retired to the country and began his last great battle. This time it was on behalf of his sister, Marjorie, who had looked after a certain Kitty Wells, a wealthy elderly relative, for more than 20 years. When Wells died it was found that she had left her considerable fortune to her solicitor, Frederick Nye. The will was hugely complex and Wintle believed it had been drawn up by Nye – the main beneficiary – to cheat Kitty Wells, who would not have been able to understand such a complicated document when she signed it.

At first Wintle simply wrote to Nye to express his concern. Nye didn't reply. Undaunted, Wintle began a campaign against the solicitor, printing gross libels about him in the local papers. There was still no response. Wintle then kidnapped Nye and took him to a hotel room. He removed the solicitor's trousers, photographed him wearing a paper dunce's hat and then turned him out – still trouserless – into the streets of Brighton. The legal profession was outraged. Wintle was arrested, found guilty of assault and sent to prison, where he was, by all accounts, enormously popular among guards and inmates. The newspapers once again had a field day and the authorities were hugely embarrassed.

When Wintle was released from Wormwood Scrubs six months later, he again went on the attack and took Nye to court. The case bankrupted Wintle but he merely observed that although he was now a pauper, he was at least an English pauper. He refused to give up. He appealed to the House of Lords, spent three days presenting his own case, and – to the astonishment of everyone – he won. The Lords argued that if they found it impossible to understand the will, it was fair to assume that when Kitty Wells was persuaded to sign it, she could not have understood it either. It was the first time a layman had represented himself and won his case in the House of Lords.

Artistic Licence –
Scandals of Bohemia

'*I am not famous;*
I am notorious.'
Quentin Crisp

SCHOOL KIDS ISSUE

4s

OZ

Vicious during his last gig at Max's, September 7

No One Is Innocent

which has
passion, i
rock 'n r
Russ Mey

The Playwright Spy
Christopher Marlowe

Christopher 'Kit' Marlowe (1564–93) was one of the greatest playwrights of the Elizabethan age. Among his works are *Dr Faustus*, *The Jew of Malta* and *Tamburlaine*, which were hugely popular in Marlowe's lifetime and have been revived continuously since his death. The public man – the author and wit – is well known to us, yet much of Marlowe's life is an enigma, and his death was surrounded by scandal, mystery and intrigue. Even today, the dark shadows that surrounded his brief life have never been fully illuminated.

The son of a shoemaker, Marlowe was born and educated in Canterbury. He must have been a remarkable child, because it was rare for someone from his background to go to university and Marlowe studied at Corpus Christi, Cambridge before setting off to make his fortune in London. We know that he was soon moving in the highest circles at court, and that he quickly earned a reputation as a poet and wit, but this is where fact ends and speculation begins.

Marlowe is said to have been in the pay of one of Queen Elizabeth I's closest advisors, Sir Francis Walsingham (c. 1530–90). Walsingham was responsible for setting up a network of spies charged with keeping an eye on Catholics and other troublemakers who might be tempted to plot against the Queen. There are no surviving details about how Marlowe earned the money he was given by Walsingham or who he watched or reported on, but by the year of his death the playwright was in trouble.

The Playwrights' Feud

Thomas Kyd (1558–94), a fellow playwright, accused Marlowe of atheism and sodomy and gave evidence to the Privy Council that papers found in his room were 'fragments of a disputation touching that opinion [atheism], affirmed by Marlowe to be his'. The papers were said to confirm Marlowe's 'vile hereticall Conceiptes Denying the Deity of Jesus Christ our Savior'.

The penalty for atheism was to be burned at the stake, something Marlowe must have been aware of. It may be that Kyd, who was already in prison when he accused Marlowe, was merely trying get himself off the hook. We will never know, nor will we ever be able to substantiate claims that Marlowe was a homosexual because just a week before he was due to go before the Privy Council to answer the accusations he was killed in a pub in Deptford, south-east London.

The circumstances surrounding Marlowe's murder are as odd as virtually everything else in his life. He was playing cards with a group of friends, among whom was Ingram Frizer. When the time came to leave the tavern an argument appears to have erupted about the bill and, in the heat of the moment, Frizer pulled a knife and grappled with Marlowe who was fatally stabbed in the eye.

With that, the mysterious life of Kit Marlowe came to an end. But to this day the whiff of scandal surrounds his life – rumours persist that he wasn't killed at all but merely changed his name to William Shakespeare and continued writing. Other stories hint that he was assassinated by Walsingham's men after a dispute about his activities as a spy or that he was silenced before he could defend himself against the atheism charge before the Privy Council.

An Expert on Prostitutes
James Boswell

Without James Boswell (1740–95), Samuel Johnson (1709–84) would probably be remembered solely as the author of the first dictionary in the English language and as a minor poet. Johnson's fame as a larger-than-life character, whose conversation sparkled with wit and intelligence, can be attributed to the biography by Boswell, a man who was considered a mere gadfly and camp follower in his day and who even irritated the man he was to immortalize.

But there was more to Boswell. For when he wasn't trying to draw out Johnson's opinions on every conceivable subject, he went off on his own along Fleet Street and got up to no good – he was devoted to the pursuit of prostitutes. Each conquest was meticulously recorded in the diaries he kept between 1762 and 1763. When the diaries were first published in the early 20th century they caused outrage, even though it had always been accepted that Boswell was rather self-obsessed and that in many ways he hoped to find his own glory reflected in Johnson's life. Nevertheless, it seemed extraordinary that the author of one of the greatest books of the 18th-century, *The Life of Samuel Johnson*, should turn out to be a man who, by Victorian standards, was beyond the pale. It was this sort of entry that caused the problem:

> *I went to Love's and drank tea. I had now been some time in town without female sport. I determined to have nothing to do with whores, as my health was of great consequence to me. I went to a girl with whom I had an intrigue at Edinburgh, but my affection cooling, I had left her. I knew she was come up. I waited on her and tried to obtain my former favours, but in vain. She would by no means listen. I was really unhappy for want of women. I thought it hard to be in such a place without them. I picked up a girl in the Strand; went into a court with intention to enjoy her in*

armour. But she had none. I toyed with her. She wondered at my size, and said if I ever took a girl's maidenhead, I would make her squeak. I gave her a shilling, and had command enough of myself to go without touching her.

A few months later he was at it again:

I went to the Park, picked up a low brimstone, called myself a barber and agreed with her for sixpence, went to the bottom of the Park arm in arm, and dipped my machine in the Canal and performed most manfully. I then went as far as St. Paul's Churchyard, roaring along, and then came to Ashley's Punch-house and drank three threepenny bowls. In the Strand I picked up a little profligate wretch and gave her sixpence. She allowed me entrance. But the miscreant refused me performance. I was much stronger than her, and volens nolens pushed her up against the wall. She however gave a sudden spring from me; and screaming out, a parcel of more whores and soldiers came to her relief. 'Brother soldiers,' said I, 'should not a half-pay officer roger for sixpence? And here has she used me so and so.' I got them on my side, and I abused her in blackguard style, and then left them. At Whitehall I picked up another girl, to whom I called myself a highwayman and told her I had no money and begged she would trust me. But she would not.

The Womanizer of the Borders
Robert Burns

The son of a poor Scottish farmer, Robert Burns (1759–96) is the most celebrated of all Scottish poets. Most of his greatest poems are love songs and, by all accounts, Burns knew a great deal about love – indeed the scandal that surrounded him was that he devoted as much time and energy to the pursuit of the lassies as he did to the pursuit of his muse. His life was a tangled mess of love affairs, and his reputation as a womanizer at least equals his reputation as a poet.

Burns had nine legitimate children and countless illegitimate offspring and, like many a modern rock star, he used his fame to gain access to as many women as possible. The first really important woman in Burns's life was Jean Armour, who he met when he was 25 and she was just 17. It wasn't long before Jean became pregnant, and although the two agreed to marry – and Jean carried a legally binding letter to this effect – Burns continued to see

ABOVE: *Robert Burns, the pursuer of the lassies.*

other women and he already had at least one illegitimate child. Jean's parents were furious when they discovered their daughter was pregnant, and they ordered her to go and live in Paisley, which was well out of Burns's way. The poet saw this as a green light to do exactly as he chose, despite a legal action initiated by Jean's parents for breach of promise.

Highland Mary and Marriage At Last

Burns soon became besotted with a 21-year-old dairymaid named Mary Campbell. Burns called her his 'Highland Mary' and wrote some of his greatest verse for her. There is some evidence that Burns now promised to marry Mary, despite his earlier promise to Jean. He may even have gone through

> ### 'Let them cant about decorum
> ### Who have characters to lose'
>
> *Robert Burns*

some sort of wedding ceremony with her, but Mary died in 1786 while giving birth to Burns's child.

Meanwhile, Jean gave birth to twins in the same year. Burns somehow got back together with her and she became pregnant again – with another set of twins! But Burns had moved on again, and was now embroiled in the last great love affair of his life – with Agnes McLehose. Agnes was already married – though separated – and all the evidence suggests that Burns was never able to seduce her. But her refusal simply fuelled his passion.

During this period, Burns had at least one other child by a woman called Jenny Clow before returning to Jean again. He was still writing love letters to Agnes and comparing Jean unfavourably to her when – out of the blue – he finally married Jean, claiming that he was entranced by her ability to produce twins! Jean was more philosophical about her part of the bargain: 'Our Robbie should have had two wives!' Jean gave birth to her last child – number nine – on the day her husband was buried.

The Opium Generation
Samuel Taylor Coleridge and Thomas De Quincey

It's hard to imagine now, but throughout the 19th and well into the 20th century, drug taking was perfectly legal. Queen Victoria famously took large quantities of opium, and as late as the 1930s a concoction known as Daffy's Elixir was sold in shops and chemists throughout England. The substance, which was designed to keep babies quiet and happy, was actually a form of liquid opium known as laudanum.

It was only in the second half of the 20th century that drug-taking became associated with subversive lifestyles – the beat generation and hippies, for example – and it was this that led to such substances being made illegal. In earlier times, the idea that something that made you feel as good as opium did should be banned would have struck people as madness, particularly in an age in which there was no anaesthetic. What is amazing is how widespread opium-taking was, despite its known health hazards.

De Quincey's Dependence

Perhaps the most famous 'artistic' drug-takers – serious addicts would be a better description – of the early 19th century were the poet Samuel Taylor

Coleridge (1772–1834) and the writer Thomas de Quincey (1785–1859), whose book *Confessions of an English Opium Eater* shocked his contemporaries. It was the first of a whole host of books that focused on the effect of drugs on the artistic temperament. Here is De Quincey comparing his favourite drug with wine:

> *Crude opium, I affirm peremptorily, is incapable of producing any state of body at all resembling that which is produced by alcohol: and not in degree only incapable, but even in kind: it is not in the quantity of its effects merely, but in the quality, that it differs altogether. The Pleasure given by wine is always mounting, and tending to a crisis, after which it declines: that from opium, when once generated, is stationary for eight or ten hours: the first, to borrow a technical distinction from medicine, is a case of acute – the second, of chronic pleasure: the one is a flame, the other a steady and equable glow. But the main distinction lies in this, that whereas wine disorders the mental faculties, opium, on the contrary (if taken in a proper manner), introduces amongst them the most exquisite order, legislation, and harmony. Wine robs a man of his self-possession: opium greatly invigorates it.*

De Quincey spent years as a serious opium addict, but it took away his appetite, brought on depression if he went a day without it and finally began to take over his life. That he should explain all this in a widely circulated publication simply confirmed in the minds of the general population that artists were a debauched bunch who should be avoided by all decent people – although of course they still read the book! Perhaps De Quincey's most outrageous confession, at least from our perspective, was his estimate that three-quarters of the population were opium takers if not addicts.

Coleridge's Addiction

Samuel Taylor Coleridge was equally passionate about opium, although it frequently made him incredibly depressed, and he was often constipated. On a ship travelling to the Mediterranean this latter ailment was so acute that the ship's surgeon had to administer an enema – a humiliation from which Coleridge never fully recovered. Complete collapse followed in 1808 as a result of the huge doses of opium he was taking every night before bed.

The hallucinations brought on by his drug-taking were terrifying, but if he didn't take his usual dose his agonies were even greater. The drug also made him self-pitying and, like a modern addict, he was constantly promising to give up his addiction but failing. Eventually, opium stopped him from being able to work at all, yet one of his most famous poems, 'Khubla Khan', was almost certainly inspired by an opium-induced dream. It clearly has all the marks of hallucination, as this extract shows:

> *A damsel with a dulcimer*
> *In a vision once I saw :*
> *It was an Abyssinian maid,*
> *And on her dulcimer she played,*
> *Singing of Mount Abora.*
> *Could I revive within me*
> *Her symphony and song,*
> *To such a deep delight 'twould win me,*
> *That with music loud and long,*
> *I would build that dome in air,*
> *That sunny dome! Those caves of ice!*
> *And all who heard should see them there,*
> *And all should cry, Beware! Beware!*
> *His flashing eyes, his floating hair!*
> *Weave a circle round him thrice,*
> *And close your eyes with holy dread,*
> *For he on honey-dew hath fed,*
> *And drunk the milk of Paradise.*

The Radical Romantic
Percy Bysshe Shelley

The great Romantic poets of the late 18th and early 19th centuries had a bad reputation for their rebellious views and outrageous behaviour. As a young man, for example, William Wordsworth (1770–1850) supported the French Revolution and fathered an illegitimate child with his French lover, Annette Vallon. However, Wordsworth lived long enough to mellow and become more conservative in his views. By comparison, Lord Byron (see pages 25–7), Percy Bysshe Shelley (1792–1822) and John Keats (1795–1821) lived short lives, and their radical credentials were unsullied by later doubts. Of the three, Shelley was in many ways the most radical. His views on almost everything scandalized English society to the point where he had to leave the country.

A Free-Thinker

Shelley was born in Sussex, the son of an MP who supported moves towards Catholic Emancipation but was in other ways fairly conventional. Everyone assumed Shelley would follow his father into Parliament, but two things changed all that. First, he met Sir Francis Burdett, an MP whose habit of mind was to question everything; second, he began to read the works of men such as Tom Paine and William Godwin while studying at Oxford. Inspired by the revolution in France, Paine and Godwin believed in universal suffrage and human rights at a time when such ideas were viewed as extremely subversive. Paine's 1791 publication *The Rights of Man* was burned in the street by the public hangman. For Shelley, Paine's work was revelatory and spurred him into action. While still at Oxford, he published articles defending the booksellers who had been imprisoned for selling books by Godwin and Paine. In 1811, Shelley and his friend T.J. Hogg (1792–1862) wrote and published a pamphlet called 'The Necessity of Atheism'. Both men were immediately sent down from Oxford.

Shelley then eloped with 16-year-old Harriet Westbrook. The ensuing scandal had nothing to do with her age, but more to do with the fact that her father was the proprietor of a coffeehouse and therefore Shelley's social inferior. Ostracized by his family, Shelley set off for Ireland where he continued to publish work in support of the French Revolution and freedom of thought.

Back in England Shelley met William Godwin (1756–1836) whose work he had so admired while at Oxford. He also met the writer Leigh Hunt (1784–1859), offering him support when he was imprisoned for writing an article that criticized the Prince Regent.

Poems on Atheism

In addition to his radical pamphleteering, Shelley wrote poetry. In 1813, he published *Queen Mab*, which further enraged polite society as it advocated free love, vegetarianism and atheism. By 1814, Shelley had left England with William Godwin's daughter, Mary (1797–1851), with whom he had fallen in love. They were accompanied by Mary's stepsister, Claire Clairmont, who became one of Byron's conquests.

Shelley continued to write and publish – one pamphlet proposed that education for the poorer sections of society should be improved and that a national referendum on electoral reform should be held. After hearing about the Peterloo Massacre in 1819, during which the Army attacked a crowd of people demonstrating peacefully in favour of electoral reform and killed 11, Shelley wrote *The Mask of Anarchy*, which placed the blame for Peterloo on the administration of Lord Castlereagh, Lord Eldon and Lord Sidmouth. Had Shelley been in England when this was published he would most certainly have been imprisoned.

Shelley never gave up his radical writing. By 1822, he and Mary were living in Italy, as was fellow radical and poet Lord Byron. The two men published a regular journal called *The Liberal*, which must have been a continual thorn in the side of the British Establishment. The publication was hugely popular – each edition of about 4,000 copies sold out and this was in a period when the nearest thing to a national newspaper sold about 1,500 copies.

Shelley's life ended in tragedy when he set sail across the Bay of Naples to visit Leigh Hunt and his boat capsized in a storm. The poet, who might have had a chance of survival if he had been able to swim, was drowned. His friends cremated his body on a nearby beach.

Ruskin's Romance
John Ruskin

A genuine polymath who inspired the artistic and literary tastes of a generation, John Ruskin (1819–1900) was a brilliant but tragic figure whose astonishing naivety led to one of the great scandals of the age.

Ruskin was influenced hugely by his mother, who was fiercely ambitious for her son. At the age of 11, he wrote a remarkably mature 200-word poem and was already a skilled draughtsman. As a young man he championed the art of J.M.W. Turner (1775–1851) and later of the Pre-Raphaelites. He was also a great social reformer – he founded the Working Men's College in 1854 and championed the establishment of pensions, free schools and public libraries long before such things were generally thought of. He was also a friend of Octavia Hill (1838–1912) who, inspired by Ruskin, later helped to found the National Trust.

Yet Ruskin's intense academic upbringing, his mother's emphasis on the life of the mind and her dislike of anything to do with the body had serious effects on her son. When he married Euphemia (Effie) Gray in 1848 he imagined that she would resemble the smooth marble statues of ancient Greece and Rome that he so admired. However, six years later the marriage was annulled on the grounds that it had never been consummated. The public trial must have been intensely embarrassing for Ruskin, as it was revealed that he was horrified to discover that his wife had pubic hair.

The case undoubtedly contributed to Ruskin's later psychological problems. Despite his international reputation as an art critic, social reformer and architectural writer, he was almost permanently unhappy and after moving to the Lake District he became increasingly reclusive. He was constantly falling in love with young girls, and his last love, Rose La Touche, who was 11 when he first met her, served merely to increase his unhappiness. He died in 1900 at Brantwood, his house on Coniston Water in the Lake District.

Wild Wilde
Oscar Wilde

The story of Oscar Wilde's (1854–1900) downfall has been told so often that there must seem little to add, but the story is unusual in that his utter condemnation was eventually to make him a hero, and ultimately his downfall did much to bolster his enduring fame. Wilde would always have been renowned as a great writer of course, but his martyrdom – which is how his downfall eventually came to be seen – made him doubly famous.

Today, the arrest and trial of Wilde seems incredibly vindictive. It whipped up a mass hysteria and orgy of self-righteousness typical of the worst excesses of the Victorian age.

A Fatal Message

The sorry tale began with the delivery of a card from the Marquess of Queensberry, who was the father of Wilde's lover Lord Alfred 'Bosie' Douglas. Queensberry was a violent, vindictive individual and vehemently objected to his son's attachment to a man who espoused the cause of the aesthetes, an Oxford group that rejected the values of the 'hearties' – the sportsmen who drank, boxed and rowed and were proud of these masculine pursuits. Wilde and his friends lived for art and beauty – and Queensberry despised them for it.

The offending card accused the dramatist of being a sodomite – although Queensberry, being virtually illiterate, mis-spelled it 'somdomite'. Wilde would probably have ignored the card, but Lord Alfred Douglas, who hated his father, saw a chance to settle a few scores and encouraged Wilde to sue. It was the biggest mistake of Wilde's life.

> *'To get back my youth I would do anything in the world, except take exercise, get up early, or be respectable.'*
>
> Oscar Wilde

Wilde had spent years mocking the Establishment world represented by the judge who presided over the case, which was inevitably biased against the effete playwright. However, evidence did suggest that Wilde had enjoyed a number of homosexual liaisons, although it was the idea of male beauty and companionship that Wilde was really in love with. This cut no ice with the court and Queensberry was found not guilty. The court was satisfied that his accusation against Wilde was true. The tables were turned and Wilde was arrested and held on remand.

ABOVE: *Oscar Wilde, before his fall from grace.*

Wilde's Nightmare

At Wilde's trial a number of working-class boys gave evidence that he had paid them to have sex with him. Even allowing for the fact that the boys were probably bribed to give evidence by Queensberry's men, Wilde was probably technically guilty under the law as it then stood. When the verdict went against him Wilde was sent to prison for two years with hard labour. It destroyed him. After his imprisonment, his plays were no longer performed; no bookshop would sell his books; and those who had copies – even signed copies – of his work destroyed, hid them or pasted labels over the author's name.

When Wilde was released from prison in 1897 he knew he had to leave England, and he left for the Continent almost immediately. He was spat at when he boarded the boat train at Victoria Station and had to change his name when he reached France, calling himself Sebastian Melmoth. His former lover and the cause of his downfall – Lord Alfred Douglas – continued to see Wilde, but less often. Wilde's only real friend was Robert Ross, who did more than anyone to help the beleaguered writer during the latter part of his life and spent years trying to restore his good name.

Wilde died a broken man in 1900. By the 1920s, his plays were once again being performed, but so deep was the scandal that Wilde's old school in Ireland only restored his name to its roll of honour in the 1950s.

Wilde's Legacy

After the scandal, Wilde's two sons, Cyril and Vyvyan, lived a life of miserable exile and were forced to change their names. Ultimately, the controversy and the destruction of one of the English language's greatest writers did a huge amount to increase sympathy for homosexuals and to bring about a change in the law. Wilde's son Vyvyan Holland's poignant memoir, which was published in the 1950s, reveals just how far-reaching the scandal was, as he described how he and his brother were hounded from one part of Europe to another.

A Life of Exile
Somerset Maugham

Despite being the best paid author of the first half of the 20th century, Somerset Maugham (1874–1965) was a deeply unhappy man. On the face of it, this makes no sense as he apparently had everything – vast wealth, a beautiful house in the south of France that was filled with valuable paintings and antiques and the freedom to travel whenever and wherever he chose.

But Maugham viewed his homosexuality as the great tragedy of his life, and he never came to terms with it. As a wealthy writer he had the freedom to indulge his tastes, and he and his lovers regularly passed young boys

'Impropriety is the soul of wit.'

Somerset Maugham

around between them. But this was the early part of the 20th century, and homosexuality was still illegal and the long shadow of Oscar Wilde's imprisonment still darkened the lives of gay men. In 1917, Maugham married Syrie Wellcome, but the union was a mistake; he grew to hate his wife and divorced her.

In the mid-1920s Maugham's homosexuality came close to being publicly revealed; he was promiscuous and there was a real risk that he would be exposed or blackmailed. Luckily for Maugham, when things looked particularly bad his brother, a high court judge who had no time for his sibling's lifestyle, warned him to leave the country. Maugham set off for France leaving a trail of rumours in his wake.

His homosexuality was an open secret among his acquaintances, and although living in France released him from fear in some ways, it didn't make him happy. What was perceived as a shameful life, which he shared with his lovers Gerald Haxton and later Alan Searle, resulted in permanent exile for the writer. He travelled almost continually from 1926 when he left Britain until his death in 1965, but he once said that he could not remember a single day when he'd felt happy.

The Artist Who Slept with Everyone
Augustus John

Augustus John (1878–1961) was without question the most bohemian artist of the last two centuries. As a young man he was considered a genius, such was his skill as a draughtsman, but his reputation waned as the 20th century progressed and the Modern Movement left him high and dry. Nevertheless, the press and the public never tired of hearing the scabrous tales of his life.

After leaving the Slade, John travelled around England and France in a horse and cart with a group of gypsies. He married Ida Nettleship in 1901, but she died in childbirth seven years later after bearing five children. John was neither faithful to her, nor was he faithful to his second long-term partner Dorelia McNeill with whom he lived on and off until his death in 1961.

John was consumed by his passion for the opposite sex – he painted many famous women, and he always made it a rule to try to seduce them, a habit he kept until he was in his late 70s. He had at least nine acknowledged offspring, but probably many more. He was also a fearless street fighter – if anyone said the wrong thing he would challenge them to a fight. On occasion even professional heavies came off worse after a fight with John.

Despite the fact that his outrageous behaviour was well known, he was fêted by society. He was the early 20th-century equivalent of a rock star – handsome, rich, famous and enormously talented: his bohemian credentials were there for all to see. It was as if his irresistible reputation was the very

BELOW: *AUGUSTUS JOHN WAS NOT ONLY AN ACCLAIMED ARTIST, BUT A FEARLESS STREET-FIGHTER.*

thing that made him irresistible – if you hadn't slept with Augustus John you hadn't arrived.

During visits to country houses, John would wander uninvited into women's bedrooms during the night. And one artist's model describes how he lurched over to her and simply lay on top of her. All she remembered was the smell of tobacco – it was all over in a minute. Even the ultra-respectable claimed to know someone who knew or had slept with Augustus John. In a bizarre way, the association bestowed credibility and made people feel that they had embraced the modern world and thrown off the stuffy shackles of convention.

Bloomsberries
Vanessa Bell and Virginia Woolf

On the death of Sir Leslie Stephen (1832–1904), his daughters, the artist Vanessa (1879–1961) and the writer Virginia (1882–1941), decided to reject the rules and conventions of the class into which they'd been born. A number of factors made this easier than it might otherwise have been. The siblings had grown up in an intellectual family – Sir Leslie edited the vast *Dictionary of National Biography* and was openly agnostic if not an atheist – and there

was a tradition of argument and rational debate in the Stephen family.

The Bloomsbury Group

Virginia and Vanessa moved from their fashionable Kensington residence to Bloomsbury, which was deemed rather seedy at the time. The rest of their family – staid aunts and dim, ultra-conservative uncles – was shocked by this move. But for the sisters it was a statement

LEFT: *Virginia Woolf's modern ways outraged society.*

about their new lives that allowed them to escape the oppressive rules and regulations of the Victorian age.

In stark contrast to the sombre, cluttered interiors of the era that reeked of respectability, they painted their new house in Gordon Square with bright colours and decorated it with modern art. They had weekly parties at which young men mixed with unmarried, unchaperoned girls. Society was outraged and the sisters' invitations to conventional balls – which they had always hated anyway – dried up. Conversation at the Bloomsbury gatherings was deliberately designed to shock – the writer Lytton Strachey (1880–1932) once said to Vanessa during a lull in a conversation: 'Is that semen on your dress?'

In 1907, Vanessa married the art critic Clive Bell (1881–1964), while in 1912 Virginia married the writer Leonard Woolf (1880–1969). Bell had a string of mistresses, but he always remained on good terms with his wife. He also stayed – if infrequently – at Charleston, Vanessa's house in Sussex, which became an artistic colony. The house, which survives today, allowed the Bloomsberries to spend long weekends discussing art and politics. These gatherings attracted some of the most talented and radical thinkers and artists in the country, including the economist John Maynard Keynes (1883–1946), the novelist E.M. Forster (1879–1970) and the painter Duncan Grant (1885–1978), to name but a few. Grant became Vanessa's lover and their daughter Angelica was born in 1918. The intricacies of Bloomsbury relationships can be judged by the fact that David Garnett, one of Grant's numerous homosexual lovers, later married Angelica!

Novello and the Black Market
Ivor Novello

Ivor Novello (1893–1951) was one of Britain's most popular entertainers during and after the First World War. Known as 'the handsomest man in England' he was also a convicted criminal who went to prison for obtaining black market petrol. But curiously, the furore surrounding his prosecution and imprisonment did nothing to damage his career – probably because half the population of Britain knew that if they had had the chance they would have done just as he did.

Novello, whose real name was David Ivor Davies, was born in Cardiff. His mother, Clara, was a well-known singer and his father a tax collector. Clara taught her son to sing and by the time he was in his teens he was already writing and publishing songs. Novello had an extraordinarily fine voice that led to a scholarship at Magdalen Choir School in Oxford. On finishing school, he

ABOVE: *Ivor Novello misused petrol coupons during the austere ration years of World War Two.*

moved to London with his parents and his career began in earnest. In 1914, Novello wrote the song that was to make him rich and famous – *Keep the Home Fires Burning*. He was known as the Welsh prodigy and later described as the new Rudolph Valentino. He wrote a number of successful musicals, and in 1916 met Bobby Andrews who was to be his companion until Novello's death in 1951.

Black Market and Bribery

Novello appeared in both silent and talking films, but during the Second World War he became involved in a scandal that could easily have wrecked his career. In 1944, he was caught misusing petrol coupons in order to obtain fuel for his Rolls Royce. When the case came to court, Novello claimed that he had needed the petrol to get him from his country house in Berkshire to the theatre where his shows were vital in keeping up the morale of Londoners. Not surprisingly, the judge was unimpressed. The picture became bleaker when it was also discovered that Novello had tried to bribe the policeman who delivered his summons to appear at court. Novello was sent to prison for eight weeks and served four. Despite the huge newspaper coverage, the troops were delighted to see Novello when he toured the front line after his release and his song *We'll Gather Lilacs* became a huge hit. Novello remained popular until his death and thousands lined the route to the cemetery at Golders Green in North London where his remains were cremated.

An Outrageous Model
Quentin Crisp

The life of Quentin Crisp (1908–98) was almost entirely devoted to scandal. He created his own unique image, which so infuriated the population of London in the 1930s that he was regularly attacked and beaten up. But Crisp refused to make himself less conspicuous, and wore make-up, shoes that were far too small, a flouncy cravat and a big floppy hat. His hair was also very long and usually dyed purple or red. He was continually taunted and abused, but he survived to become a writer whose books sold across the world and whose life-story was made into an extremely successful film.

A Human Work of Art

Crisp was born in Sutton, a dull south London suburb. It hardly seems fair to say that his real name was Dennis Pratt, as in a very real sense he was always Quentin Crisp. At the age of 21 he left the suburbs and moved into London where he lived in a series of dingy bedsits. Here, he slowly created one of the most famous works of art of the 20th century – himself.

Crisp had been used to being beaten up at school, but that was nothing to the attacks he suffered during the dull conformist days of 1930s London. When he was later asked why he didn't simply tone down his flamboyant and feminine appearance he remarked that he had no choice. He had to be what he was and that involved being obviously effeminate. Crisp had a number of relationships, but he preferred to live alone. He spent his evenings in cafés and bars drinking tea, spending as little money as possible and talking. He was often asked to leave by café owners who were disgusted by his appearance.

Crisp also worked as a commercial artist, but was frequently sacked. Then he found a role that suited him perfectly – he was employed as a life model in state-funded art schools all over London and south-east England. This meant that he received regular pay for taking his clothes off – the perfect employment. It also inspired his 1968 book *The Naked Civil Servant*, which caused a sensation when it was published.

At the age of 72, Crisp left his homeland to live in New York saying that England was a 'mistake'. The wit and wisdom of Quentin Crisp – known in some quarters as 'Crisperanto' – became legendary. He refused ever to clean his flat, claiming that after a few years the dirt and dust didn't get any worse.

Crisp outraged both homosexuals and heterosexuals. He claimed that homosexuality was an illness. However, his blasé attitude concealed a deep melancholy. He said he wanted to die at the hands of a murderer and that he hoped his body would be placed in a black refuse sack and thrown away with all the other trash.

Having proudly claimed that he had failed at almost everything he'd done, Crisp found himself famous, and in his last years, rather than being reviled, spat at and beaten up, as he was in his youth, he was fêted as a pioneer of gay rights. Crisp became a hugely popular entertainer and continued with his one-man show into his late 80s. While visiting a friend in Manchester he collapsed and died at the grand old age of 90.

Bacon's Boys
Francis Bacon

Extraordinary stories about the painter Francis Bacon (1909–1992) and his life in Soho are legion. Bacon was central to an artistic group that met at the French House pub and the Colony Room, although he was just as often found in rough, seedy pubs all over this bohemian quarter of London.

Bacon, who received no formal art training, became the most celebrated British painter of the 20th century, and his private life was bizarre by any standards. He claimed that his taste for rough homosexual sex began when his father asked the stable lads on his family's estate in Ireland to whip him on the bare buttocks. Although he hated the humiliation at the time, he said it gave him a taste for brutality – a taste that also informed his art.

Bacon was constantly ill as child, which aroused no sympathy in his stern military-minded father. Various attempts to make a real man of the young Bacon merely worsened the relationship between father and son. In 1925, the discovery that Francis was homosexual – he was caught wearing his sister's clothes – ended the painter's relationship with his family for good.

Bacon travelled to Berlin with a family friend who promptly seduced him and introduced him to the decadent delights of the Weimar Republic, the German state that existed from 1919 until Hitler's rise to power in the 1930s. It was a world that was brilliantly encapsulated in Christopher Isherwood's novel *Goodbye to Berlin*, which was later adapted as the film *Cabaret*.

Returning to England, Bacon tried to carve out a life for himself as an interior designer. He achieved some success, but gradually moved to painting and drawing, having been inspired by Picasso's work, which he'd seen at an exhibition. Bacon used photographs, films and other works of art to inspire

ABOVE: OSCAR WILDE'S FRIENDSHIP WITH LORD ALFRED DOUGLAS, OTHERWISE KNOWN AS 'BOSIE', WAS TO BE THE PLAYWRIGHT'S DOWNFALL.

ABOVE: DR CRIPPEN MADE UP DIFFERENT STORIES FOR BOTH FRIENDS AND THE POLICE TO EXPLAIN HIS WIFE CORA'S DISAPPEARANCE, WHEN IN REALITY HE HAD BUTCHERED HER.

his painting. His *Three Figures at the Base of a Crucifixion* caused outrage when it was first exhibited, but he went on to produce images of even greater brutality. Perhaps his most famous picture is that of the so-called *Screaming Pope*, a reinterpretation of Velazquez's famous 17th-century portrait of Pope Innocent X.

The Soho Clique

Throughout his career Bacon haunted Soho. He would usually begin a day there with lunch at Wheelers, where he would buy his friends champagne, and then drink the afternoon and evening away in the Colony Room or the French House before returning to his filthy, cluttered studio in the early hours to paint until dawn. He then slept until lunchtime.

Among his Soho cronies was the photographer John Deakin, who took so little care of his work that most of what survives is creased, torn, stained or damaged in some way. Daniel Farson, author of *Never a Normal Man,* was also a friend, as was John Minton, a painter who later committed suicide, and several other artists, including Lucian Freud and Frank Auerbach.

One of the best stories about Bacon's notorious life originated after one of his numerous trips to Tangier in search of boys. While there, he wandered the streets at night and was regularly beaten up and robbed. The British Consul complained to the authorities, telling them that it was an outrage that Britain's best-known painter did not receive protection. The chief of police explained patiently that they had offered Bacon a bodyguard, but he refused it on the grounds that he enjoyed being physically abused.

Bacon was in his 80s when he died, by which time his pictures were selling for as much as a £1,000,000 each. The last scandal of his life was the decision to leave his whole estate – amounting to more than £10,000,000 – to his illiterate boyfriend, John Edwards.

Celtic Cads
Dylan Thomas and Brendan Behan

An American research project has revealed that people with Celtic surnames are roughly ten times more likely to become alcoholics than others are. This may go some way towards explaining the extraordinary reputation that the Scots, Irish and Welsh have for hard drinking. Numerous Celtic writers, actors and artists fit neatly into this hard-drinking profile – for example, the hell-raising actors Richard Burton (1925–84) and Richard Harris (1932–2002). But among the most notorious of all are the Welsh poet Dylan Thomas (1914–53) and the Irish writer Brendan Behan (1923–64).

The Welsh Laureate

There is some conjecture that Thomas, who was born in Swansea, decided to play the part of the drunken poet. If it was a part, it was played supremely well, for he spent much of his life drinking heavily and died after a monumental bout of boozing in New York at the age of just 39.

Thomas's hard drinking and his brilliant poetry became the stuff of legend. He had a good start in life. Both his parents encouraged him to write – his father was a schoolmaster and frustrated poet – and Thomas's poems first appeared in his school magazine, although it was run by his father!

In 1927, Thomas sent a poem to Wales's largest circulating newspaper, the *Western Mail*, which was published, although it was later discovered that the verse was written by someone else! But the aspiring poet had a burning desire to succeed where his father had failed. In 1931, Thomas left school and got a job on the local paper. It was here that his serious boozing began. After a couple of years he left or was sacked (the story varies) and became a free-lance writer. From here on, despite his later fame, Thomas was never free from financial difficulty.

BELOW: *DYLAN THOMAS MORE THAN ENJOYED A DRINK, AND EVENTUALLY DRANK HIMSELF TO DEATH.*

He moved to London in 1934, and soon his first collection of verse *18 Poems* was published. It was highly praised, but his bouts of drunkenness did not endear him to many – when he was drunk he could be very unpleasant indeed. Over the next few years, his reputation as a poet grew rapidly, but his notoriety as a drinker and womanizer grew even faster. He moved constantly between London, where he mostly drank, and Wales where he did his best work.

In 1936, Thomas met and fell in love with Caitlin McNamara, who was certainly his match when it came to hard drinking and promiscuity. They married in 1937, and from the outset they had public shouting matches and fights, which were largely fuelled by alcohol. They were never faithful to each other, Thomas frequently tried to seduce the wives of his friends and those who helped him; most famously he slept with the wife of the Oxford academic A.J.P. Taylor. Meanwhile, Caitlin had an on-off affair with the artist Augustus John (see pages 74–6).

Thomas set off for a tour of America in 1950. Here, he was pursued by creditors and scandal in equal measure. He was fêted as a literary lion, but he was drinking more heavily than ever. A further American tour in 1953 saw him bloated, confused and unable to read his lines during a radio broadcast. He was thrown out of a theatre for disrupting the performance and later fell down a set of stairs in a drunken fit and broke his arm. In November of that year, Thomas was drinking almost continuously, despite regular vomiting. He finally lapsed into a coma and died on 9 November 1953. It was said that he loved the idea of being a drunken poet more than he loved alcohol. Typically forthright, Caitlin arrived in New York just before the poet's death and asked: 'Is the bloody man dead yet?'.

Borstal Boy

Brendan Behan's life mirrored that of Dylan Thomas, and in a way it is surprising that both men managed to achieve so much. In Thomas's case there were several collections of verse and the masterful play *Under Milk Wood*. Behan wrote the autobiographical *Borstal Boy*, *The Quare Fellow* and a number of other highly successful plays, yet legend has it that, like Thomas, he spent much of his life in an alcoholic haze.

Behan was born into a poor, working-class Dublin family, Nevertheless, reading and literature were important – Behan's mother took her children on literary tours of the city and they were also taught Irish, which Behan spoke fluently. At 13, he left school to work in his father's house-painting business and soon after he joined the IRA (Irish Republican Army), with whom he played an active part in the fight for a unified Republican Ireland. His first work was printed in *The Voice of Ireland*, a periodical published by the youth wing of the IRA. In 1939, he was sent to England with a suitcase full of explosives and promptly arrested. He was sent to borstal for three years, an experience that helped him write his classic work, *Borstal Boy*.

Behan was released in 1941, but soon fell back in with the IRA and hence returned to jail a year later for attempted murder. He was released in 1946 and then imprisoned again for a short time in Manchester for helping another prisoner escape.

By the 1950s, a string of plays and poems meant Behan could earn a living as a writer, but he was also notorious as a hard-drinking reveller. His play *The Quare Fellow* (1954) earned him an international reputation as a playwright despite his violent, criminal past. Like Thomas, he visited America where he was treated like royalty, but drank in his usual impassioned way. During the late 1950s and early 1960s his chaotic private life became more and more public as he regularly gave television and radio interviews in which he was blind drunk. During his last few years he was so ill from alcoholism that he was unable to write a thing.

Prick Up Your Ears
Joe Orton

Joe Orton (1933–1967) who was famous – or infamous – for his anarchic plays, first came to public attention when he and his lover, Kenneth Halliwell, borrowed books from Islington Library and defaced them. John Betjeman's picture was removed from a volume of his collected verse, for example, and replaced with a picture of a fat, naked man covered in tattoos. For their relatively minor crime, Halliwell and Orton were given six-month prison sentences.

Orton was born into a working-class family in Leicester, a city that he came to loathe. He failed miserably at school, but became interested in drama, and was accepted as a pupil at RADA when he was just 16 years old. Here he met Kenneth Halliwell, who was seven years his senior. Halliwell was well educated and had a small private income that supported the pair when they began to live together in north London.

Halliwell had literary ambitions and the two men collaborated on a number of novels, none of which was published. Orton eventually managed to complete a play *The Boy Hairdresser*, which was broadcast by the BBC as *The Ruffian On the Stair*. There was no looking back, and Orton produced a string of successful stage plays. The comedies, which included *Entertaining Mr Sloane* (1964) and *Loot* (1965), delighted and outraged audiences by poking fun – often obscenely – at the sort of prim suburban values that Orton had left behind in Leicester.

By early 1967, Orton's plays were being performed all over the world, but, as his career soared, Halliwell felt increasingly marginalized. He had helped to educate Orton and supported him, but he was now in danger of losing him. In August 1967, Halliwell murdered his lover and committed suicide. It was the last sad act in a drama that had been filled with scandal and heartbreak.

The Lady and The Gamekeeper
The Lady Chatterley Trial

The 'Lady Chatterley' trial was the point at which the modern world came of age and the last vestiges of Victorian England were finally routed. The essence of the old order was encapsulated in the prosecuting barrister's question to the jury – 'Would you let your wives or your servants read this?'

Published in Paris and Italy in the 1920s where no great fuss was made, *Lady Chatterley's Lover* was banned in England under the obscenity acts. The short novel by D.H. Lawrence (1885–1930) tells the story of the passionate affair between a gamekeeper called Mellors and Lady Constance Chatterley, whose husband is confined to a wheelchair. It is by no means Lawrence's best work, but it is certainly his most notorious. By the standards of the time it was highly erotic and explicit, mentioning 'swinging breasts', 'fucking' and 'the erect phallus'.

Ironically, the scandal surrounding the trial made the book a huge best-seller, but it was a trial that the publishers themselves deliberately provoked. The government had passed the Obscene Publications Act in 1959. The following year was the 30th anniversary of D.H. Lawrence's death and Penguin planned to reprint his complete works, including *Lady Chatterley's Lover*. The publisher had 200,000 copies of the book printed and stored in a warehouse before sending a dozen copies to the Director of Public Prosecutions and inviting him to bring a case against them. This he duly did.

A Challenging Read

When the case came to court in 1960, the country was split into pre-war conservatives and the post-war generation, which had grown up with very different values. The newspapers covered every detail of the trial, and the coverage in the press was so great that another book describing the trial itself was even banned!

The government had agreed that works of merit could escape prosecution if the 'merit' outweighed the obscenity and this was the basis of Penguin's defence. To back up their claim they called dozens of witnesses, including

ABOVE: *A*TTEMPTS *TO BAN* D.H. L*AWRENCE'S* L*ADY* C*HATTERLEY'S* L*OVER* *BOOSTED SALES OF THE BOOK ENORMOUSLY.*

bishops, academics and celebrated writers, among whom was the novelist E.M. Forster.

The prosecution had little to go on, which is why counsel Mervyn Griffith-Jones – in desperation – asked the jury if they would allow their wives and servants to read the book. That this never-to-be-forgotten line could be asked in the 1960s revealed just how out of step with society the Establishment was. And with this question Griffith-Jones probably did as much as anything to ensure that the defence won, as it seemed to hint at other objections to the book – objections to do with class. And there is no doubt that one of the reasons the book had originally been banned was that it involved an upper-class woman having an affair with a working-class man.

If the trial was one of the big scandals of the 1960s, the publicity produced something even more shocking – at least in the view of arch-conservatives. When it was finally published, all 200,000 copies of *Lady Chatterley's Lover* were sold in one day – solely as a result of the publicity generated by the trial.

Teenage Kicks
The Oz trial

The big surprise of the trial of the three editors of the underground hippie magazine *Oz* was not the sentencing of the three – which was out of all proportion to the offence – but rather the backlash caused by the proceedings, which led to the biggest investigation of police corruption in British history. For while Soho pornographers were tolerated by the Metropolitan Police, editors Richard Neville, Jim Anderson and Felix Dennis felt the full force of the law.

The trial took place in 1971 and came about because of claims that *Oz* magazine and similar anti-Establishment publications, corrupted young people. It centred on *Oz 28*, which had been guest-edited by a group of teenagers. It was this edition that led to the raid on the magazine's offices and the eventual prosecution of its three editors.

What the authorities disliked was that the magazine openly stated that teenagers were interested in sex and alternative lifestyles that threatened the status quo. As with the Lady Chatterley trial (see pages 85–7), what the *Oz* trial was really about was the old order trying to stay in control in the face of youthful rebellion – which explains why the three defendants were forced to have haircuts before they appeared in court!

From the Establishment's point of view, the prosecution quickly backfired – the sentences of 15 months for each defendant, which came after an appallingly biased summing up by the judge Michael Argyle, caused a public outcry and the prison sentences were almost immediately overturned on appeal. Newspapers and other commentators took up the cause of the three editors and questions emerged about the police's inaction in the face of a growing porn industry. Lord Widgery sent his clerk to buy porn in Soho and he returned with armfuls of the stuff. The material that was bought was freely available and made *Oz* magazine look completely harmless. The Home Secretary asked for an inquiry.

In The Pay Of the Porn Barons

When the police themselves were investigated for pursuing the publishers of *Oz* while allowing the Soho porn barons a free hand, all enquiries were met with a wall of silence. But the cat leapt firmly out of the bag when the head of the flying squad – Commander Kenneth Drury – was discovered on holiday in Cyprus with a well-known porn baron.

The inquiry eventually led to the jailing of the very policeman who'd brought the prosecution against the *Oz* trio. In fact, a massive inquiry uncovered corruption at all levels. In total 400 officers, including a deputy police commissioner, either left the force or were imprisoned as a result of the investigations. Detective Chief Inspector George Fenwick went to prison for ten years, after a judge decided he was the chief architect of a system of corruption that meant senior police officers were in the pay of the Soho porn barons. Fenwick's assertion that the prosecution of the *Oz* three was justified as they were advocating an alternative society cut no ice when it was his turn to face a jury.

Art Forgers Extraordinaires
Eric Hebborn and Tom Keating

Eric Hebborn (1934–96) and Tom Keating (1917–84) were two of history's greatest art forgers and when their activities were first brought to public attention a shiver of horror went through the art establishment. What is really fascinating about the story of these two men is that even today no one knows how many of the fake masterpieces they produced are still held in private and public collections and believed to be genuine. Both went to their graves without divulging the extent of their activities, but the irony is that the scandal that brought their names to public attention ultimately gave their fakes an inherent value.

Old Masters

Hebborn was born in London, but descended from an old Oxford family of showmen. His childhood was difficult – he claimed his father drank and his mother 'packed a good punch'. As a teenager he was sent to an approved school for arson, but his precocious artistic talents were recognized when he was sent to study in London and then under Anthony Blunt, the surveyor of the Queen's pictures, in Rome.

Hebborn was a brilliant artist, but he resented the fact that the art market was dominated by modern art, rather than the more considered and skilful techniques of which he was a master. Hebborn burst into the limelight when the Daily Mail ran a story on him in 1991. An article claimed that he had sold hundreds, if not thousands, of works by Old Masters, as well as paintings by Thomas Gainsborough and Nicolas Poussin. The problem was not that he'd sold them, but that they were actually his own work passed off as that of great artists. Hebborn claimed that he had done this because he disliked the accents and attitudes of those who ran the art world.

When the story was published, museums and galleries all over the world began to re-examine their collections. Even great national collections began to worry that some of their Renaissance drawings were fake, but they could not be sure. Hebborn was never specific about what he had done and he was never prosecuted. It is thought that dealers would arrive at his door and ask if he had any Old Master drawings for sale. If he said no they would go away and come back with the necessary materials!

Hebborn died in mysterious circumstances in Rome in 1996 and the extent of his forgery and its penetration of museums and collections remains unknown. He may have exaggerated his forgeries, but experts are known to have been fooled by his work on many occasions.

A Bitter Lesson

Like Hebborn, the artist and picture restorer Tom Keating was bitter at the vast sums involved in the art business and to teach the dealers a lesson he painted 13 pictures in the style of the great 18th-century English painter Samuel Palmer, and claimed they were original. He was tried at the Old Bailey in 1976, where it was claimed he had painted more than 2,000 works that were then falsely attributed to more than 100 different artists. The trial was halted because Keating was ill and he died before it could resume.

In truth, no one in the art establishment wanted Keating or Hebborn put on trial, as no one really wanted to discover if their pictures were fakes. The loss of reputation among the experts would have been unbearable, not to mention the serious loss of confidence in the market.

Both Keating and Hebborn would have been delighted when – in another huge scandal in the 1990s – it was revealed that Christie's and Sotheby's had been operating an illegal cartel to drive up prices. The master forgers would no doubt have enjoyed saying 'We told you so!'.

Beatles and Bishops
Rock'n'Rollers

From the Jazz Age onwards, musicians were known for their bohemian, drug-taking lifestyle, but rather than flaunt it they tended to keep it very much in their private lives. By the early 1960s that had all changed, and the desire to enjoy the notoriety that shocking people brought – not to mention the enhanced record sales – meant that leading a wild, drink- and drug-filled life became an essential element of a rock star's persona. Without some hint of scandal a rock star was unlikely to become or remain a star.

Perhaps the biggest rock'n'roll scandal of the 1960s was the Beatles' announcement that they were more famous than Jesus, which briefly caused youngsters all over the United Kingdom and America to start throwing their records away or burning them. Then there was the imprisonment on drugs charges of the Rolling Stones' wild boy Keith Richards. Richards' house had been searched and a small amount of cannabis found. However, the biggest fuss to emerge from that raid wasn't the drug bust itself, but the presence of Marianne Faithfull and what she was alleged to have been doing with a Mars bar!

BELOW: *MARIANNE FAITHFULL, WHOSE ALLEGED ACTIONS WITH A MARS BAR GAINED HER NOTORIETY.*

For the older generation the whole hippie movement of the 1960s, which was intimately tied up with popular music, was a rejection of everything they stood for. Elderly generals appeared on television to denounce bands such as The Grateful Dead, and bishops attacked their music in the mistaken belief that it was likely to encourage people towards Satanism. By 1969, the dream of flower power had degenerated into an orgy of self-indulgent pseudo mysticism and drug-taking. The symbolic end to the great experiment of peace and free love seemed to come with the Rolling Stones' concert at Altamont when one fan was beaten to death by a group of Hell's Angels employed to keep order.

Throughout the 1970s and 1980s, rock stars struggled with their drug habits. It became standard procedure for rock stars to smash up hotels in the manner of The Who's Keith Moon or die of an overdose in the manner of Janis Joplin or Jim Morrison. Rock stars were expected to father numerous children with various women as Mick Jagger has done. But what was outrageous behaviour in the 1960s aroused almost no comment by the 1990s. Rock'n'roll and its accompanying lifestyle had become the musical equivalent of the City suit. You might not like it, but it was the uniform of the trade. And although bands such as Oasis tried to emulate the heady heights of notoriety achieved in the 1960s and 1970s, it always seemed as if they were trying a little too hard.

Masterminds,
Murderers and Misers –
Fraudsters and Freaks

'I don't think of myself as a criminal. I was trying to correct a situation.'

Nick Leeson

Soldier of Fortune
Thomas Blood

One of the greatest scandals of the 17th century was the attempted theft of the Crown Jewels. No one thought it was possible, yet it was achieved by an Irishman who so charmed King Charles II once he was caught that he was not only pardoned, but given land in Ireland and awarded a pension.

Thomas Blood (c. 1618–80) was born in Mayo in the west of Ireland. He was a soldier of fortune who came to England in the 1640s to fight for King Charles I during the English Civil War. However, when he realized that Charles was going to lose, he switched sides. After the war, Blood became a respected figure in the Commonwealth government. When Cromwell died and Charles II returned from his French exile in 1660, Blood knew he was a marked man and fled to Ireland.

Blood was never happier than when he was involved in a conspiracy, so it was no surprise when he teamed up with a group of exiled Parliamentarians and tried to kidnap the governor of Dublin Castle. The kidnap attempt failed and Blood fled to Holland. He assumed an alias and returned to England in 1670, where he began to plan the robbery that was to be the sensation of the age.

An Audacious Plan

Dressed as a clergyman, Blood visited the Tower of London with his wife. The keeper of the Crown Jewels, Talbot Edwards, allowed him to view the treasures and then Blood made as if to leave. Mrs Blood then pretended to faint and was helped by the jewel-keeper's wife. This gave Blood the excuse to return to the Tower a few days later with a gift of thanks for Mrs Edwards. He made every effort to befriend the Edwards family and was largely successful. The two families became close and Blood suggested that his nephew should marry Edwards' daughter.

The wedding discussion took place in a room above the underground cellar where the jewels were kept. Blood turned up with his supposed nephew – in fact a co-conspirator – and two other family friends. While the nephew kept the daughter and mother in one room, Edwards took Blood and his two friends to see the jewels. As soon as the iron door to the jewel room had been opened Edwards was hit over the head and cut with a sword. While he was unconscious the three men flattened the orb and crown and stuffed them inside their clothes. The thieves almost escaped, but Edwards came round and raised the alarm. Blood was captured as he left the Tower.

In the aftermath of the crime, Blood refused to speak to anyone but the King. His charm was legendary, but no one thought that he could talk his way out of this. However, Charles was immediately taken with Blood; he asked him: 'What if I should give you your life?', to which Blood replied 'I should endeavour to deserve it.' To the astonishment of his courtiers, Charles pardoned Blood and granted him land in Ireland.

The Stock Market Stampede
The South Sea Bubble

The scandal of the South Sea Company and its eventual collapse had as much to do with greed and hysteria as with a deliberate attempt to defraud. It started as an apparently sensible means to service Britain's national debt and ended as the biggest financial disaster in the nation's history.

It all began in 1711 when the government granted the South Sea Company exclusive rights to trade with Spanish South America. In return, the company took on almost £10,000,000 of government debt. The company had been founded in the hope that the War of the Spanish Succession, which had raged since 1701, would quickly come to an end, thus allowing a vast increase in trade to and from Spanish South America. In fact, the conflict did not end until 1713 and further conflict broke out in 1718. This meant the company actually did very little trade with South America. Therefore, in order to pay the promised levels of interest to their existing stockholders, it had to sell increasing amounts of stock, but it was stock based on the hope of future trade not on actual trade – which was minimal.

In 1719, the company took on a further two-thirds of Britain's National Debt, which amounted to more than £7,000,000 – billions by today's standards. Taking on more debt increased public confidence and even more stock was sold. The directors of the South Sea Company managed to convince individuals that their stock would be worth a fortune and people began to invest in a frenzy of excitement. In a short time share values rose almost tenfold. As hysteria grew, a large number of companies were set up independently of the South Sea Company deliberately to defraud investors – such was the buying fever, people could be persuaded to invest in all kinds of absurd schemes, among which was a plan to make cannons to fire square cannonballs.

Trading in Air

Despite their extravagant claims for future success, the directors of the South Sea Company knew they were only able to pay existing stockholders by selling new stock. It was a spiral that was bound to end in disaster. Between June and September of 1720, the price of stock rose to 1,000 and then

ABOVE: *The South Sea Bubble was possibly the most extraordinary financial scandal of all time; caused by greed and hysteria, it devastated thousands of lives.*

plummeted to 150. As it fell, investors panicked and couldn't sell their stock fast enough. What had been a run on stock turned into a collapse. Vast fortunes were lost in a day. Thousands, including many wealthy landowners, were ruined as the South Sea Bubble burst; even banks collapsed.

In December, Parliament was recalled to discuss the issue and former Chancellor of the Exchequer Robert Walpole (1676–1745), who'd always distrusted the scheme, was called in to sort out the mess. But still the bankruptcies continued; dozens committed suicide, including the post-master general. Families that had known great wealth never recovered. The directors of the South Sea Company were arrested and their land and property confiscated. More than 500 members of the Houses of Parliament lost money; the then chancellor, John Aislabie, was forced to resign in disgrace and the Royal Family was spat at as they drove through the streets. It was, in short, the financial scandal to end them all.

The Resurrection Men
Burke and Hare

As science advanced in the 18th century, medical schools needed bodies to study. However, in those days no respectable person donated their body to science in the modern manner as it was viewed as sacrilege. The bodies of hanged men were taken for dissection, but the demand for corpses far exceeded supply. With good money paid for fresh bodies and questions rarely asked, a flourishing business began, particularly in Edinburgh.

The recently deceased were a valuable commodity and the so-called resurrection men got to work. These individuals kept an eye out for funerals, visited graveyards the night after burials and dug up corpses, selling them on for anything between £7 and £10 each. These sums were small fortunes in the 18th century and little could be done to prevent the thefts. Some families mounted round-the-clock guards on relatives' graves for days after a burial, but when that was not possible the dead were vulnerable.

The Body Snatchers

The most famous resurrection men, William Burke (1792–1829) and William Hare (1790–1859), took the process of supplying bodies to science a gruesome step further. The first body they sold had died a natural death, but having been paid handsomely for its delivery the pair became greedy and impatient. They were soon carefully selecting weak individuals as victims and smothering them in such a way that signs of foul play were difficult to spot.

It is believed that Burke and Hare killed and sold as many as 16 people in this way before a lodger in Hare's house spotted a body and raised the alarm. The men were arrested, but there was little hard evidence to convict them – they claimed their latest victim had died of natural causes. As there was no

ABOVE: *William Burke on the scaffold in 1829. Burke may have murdered as many as 16 people in order to sell their bodies for scientific experiments.*

proof, nothing could be done, until Hare was persuaded to turn Queen's evidence. As a result, Burke was tried and hanged.

More than 100,000 thousand people are said to have come to Edinburgh from all over Scotland to see the condemned man die and there were cheers as he was led to the scaffold. One witness described it as a great holiday and celebration. After the execution it was weeks before Hare could be spirited out of the city – so great was the sense of outrage, he would have been lynched if he'd tried to leave without being heavily disguised. He was never seen or heard of again, and was lucky to escape with his life. Such was the scandal associated with the resurrection men that the law was changed. The Anatomy Act of 1832 allowed surgeons to claim the bodies of those who died without family in local workhouses. The price for dead bodies fell and, without a ready market, the resurrection men vanished from history.

A Victorian Train Robber
Edward Agar

When people think of the Great Train Robbery, the crude, bungled heist of 1963 springs to mind (see pages 108–9), but that incident was nothing compared to the Great Train Robbery of 1855. When the mastermind behind the 19th-century crime was eventually caught – and his capture had nothing to do with his failure to execute the robbery – even the judge described him as a genius.

A Career Criminal

The genius in question was Edward Agar. Little is known about his life before he became famous for his scandalous exploits on the London to Folkestone railway, but these exploits were such that they undermined confidence in the banking system across Europe. By his own admission a career criminal, Agar had amassed a small fortune before deciding to risk everything on the most daring crime of his career. Although he was in his 40s at the time of the crime, he had never once before been caught for any offence.

An Impossible Crime

Agar was acquainted with a barrister by the name of Saward, a corrupt lawyer who had turned to crime to pay his gambling debts. Saward was friendly with a fellow called Pierce who had been sacked from the South Eastern Railway for his addiction to gambling. When Pierce heard from his former railway colleagues that huge loads of gold bullion were regularly carried from London to Folkestone by train – from whence they were ferried across the English Channel and then on to Paris – he suggested to Saward that they steal one of the shipments. Saward turned to Agar, the greatest safe-breaker of the age, to see if it could be done.

Agar had carved out a flawless criminal career through meticulous research and preparation. This attention to detail enabled him to make some startling discoveries about the gold shipments. The gold was carried in a solid-steel safe that was made by Chubb (who were famous for making impregnable safes) and fitted with locks that were said to be unpickable. There were two sets of keys: one set was held by the stationmaster at London Bridge, from where the trains departed, the other set by the stationmaster at Folkestone. Inside the inch-thick steel of the safe, the gold was stored in locked bullion chests, which also carried the bank's seals. The seals were checked before departure, again at Folkestone and finally when they reached their destination in Paris, where two further keys to the safe were held. Agar concluded that the robbery was totally impossible and told Saward so.

A Lucky Break

That seemed to be the end of the matter, until fortune intervened and changed everything. Agar's mistress was friendly with James Burgess, a guard on the South Eastern Railway. Burgess was disgruntled at the decline in railwaymen's wages since the railway boom had ended. He quickly became a co-conspirator, as did one William Tester, a superintendent's assistant at London Bridge.

However, the accident of fortune that made the robbery possible was the railway company's loss of one of their two keys to the train safe. The company's directors were so worried about this that they sent the safe back to Chubb and new locks and keys were fitted. The correspondence about the work passed through the hands of Tester, who slipped out of the office with the new keys on the day they were returned from Chubb and met Agar in a nearby pub, where the master criminal took an impression of the keys in a tin of wax.

Then came a setback. Tester had brought two copies of the same key, which meant that the other was still beyond the conspirators' reach in Folkestone. To procure it, Agar travelled to Folkestone one evening and walked along the platform to the little office where the key was kept. When the office closed he smoked the office's lock using a narrow, hollow metal cylinder that had been split in two lengthways and blackened with candle-smoke. Agar slid the two halves of the cylinder into the lock until they covered the central spindle of the mechanism. Once inserted the two halves of the cylinder were turned and then carefully removed. Clearly marked in the smoke-blackened areas of metal was the outline of the lock's levers. Using this Agar had a key made that would open the lock.

Knowing that gold was carried in the Chubb safe on the mail train, Agar sent himself a box of gold sovereigns to be collected at the Folkstone office. When he went to collect his sovereigns, the stationmaster, seeing a highly respectable figure standing before him, didn't hesitate before unlocking a small cabinet on the wall, taking out the key to the safe and setting off for the train to collect Agar's gold. In the ten minutes he was gone, Agar made a wax impression of the cabinet's lock. He then collected his gold and left.

Later that night Agar returned to the office, opened the cabinet and took an impression of the second Chubb key. He now had both keys to the impregnable safe. To make sure the copies would work, Burgess let Agar into the guards' van of the London Bridge to Folkestone mail train on a night when it was stationary. Here, Agar tried the keys and filed them until they worked perfectly.

The Perfect Crime

On 15 May 1855, the robbery began. Pierce climbed aboard the mail train at London Bridge carrying two carpetbags, each of which contained a hundredweight of lead shot. The bags were taken to the guards' van where the Chubb safe was kept. Agar deliberately waited until he'd almost missed the train then leapt aboard the guards' van – just as any late-running passenger might – as Burgess waved his flag for the off.

The journey from London Bridge to Redhill, which was the train's first stop, gave Agar just over half an hour. He immediately opened the safe, and using specially prepared pincers and thin levers, he eased up the rivets on the steel bands of the bullion chests. With the bands loosened a fraction he was able to drive wedges between the lid of the chest and the base until the lock burst in such a way that the seal was left intact. This meant that on casual inspection at Folkestone all would seem well.

Before the train reached Redhill, Agar had removed the gold from one chest and weighed out exactly the same amount of lead shot, which he placed in the bullion chest. The rivets were knocked back into place, the chest was replaced in the safe and it was locked. The bag was then discreetly passed to Tester when the train stopped. It contained nearly 40lb of solid gold bullion. Meanwhile Pierce, who'd been travelling first class, got off the train, walked along the platform and jumped into the guards' van.

The train headed for Tonbridge next, and Agar emptied the second bullion chest. Just as before, the precious cargo was replaced with exactly the same weight of lead shot, the chest was re-sealed and replaced in the safe. The same was repeated for the third chest. By the time they reached Tonbridge the two men had more than two-hundredweight of gold, which was secreted in bags strapped to their chests and in the carpetbags. Just before 11pm the train reached Folkestone. The men left the guards' van and walked along the platform before re-boarding the train. At Dover they went back to the guards' van and collected the carpetbags. They remained at a local hotel for a short time before catching the next train back to London. Within a few hours some of the gold had already been turned into currency that couldn't be traced and the theft had still not been discovered. The chests passed examination at Folkestone and Boulogne. It was not until the following afternoon when they were opened in Paris that the robbery was discovered. The banks involved immediately sued the South Eastern Railway, which refused to pay up on the grounds that the robbery must have been carried out in France. Of course, the French railway service denied everything. But everyone agreed that the robbery was impossible.

Meanwhile Agar and Pierce melted the gold down at a house in Kilburn and disposed of it through the corrupt barrister Saward.

Framed

Agar was caught more than a year later, although he was arrested on an entirely different matter, having been framed by a criminal associate after falling for the man's girlfriend. The crime was forgery and Agar's enemies gave evidence against him. He knew he would be transported to Australia for at least 20 years so he wrote to Pierce asking him to use some of the money from the train robbery to look after his ex-mistress and their child. However, Pierce cheated Agar's former lover, and when the mastermind found out he decided to give Queen's evidence against his former colleagues and reveal all about the robbery that had baffled the British and French police for more than a year.

Pierce was sentenced to two years hard labour and Tester and Burgess were transported for 14 years. Agar's sentence for forgery stood, but because he had not been found guilty of the train robbery neither his wealth nor that of his associates could be taken from him and so all of it – millions of pounds in today's money – went to Agar's ex-girlfriend and his child. And with that, Agar, perhaps the greatest of all British criminals, disappeared from history.

The Whitechapel Murders
Jack the Ripper

The terror and sensation surrounding the Jack the Ripper murders was huge. For someone who killed so often and in a relatively small area not to be caught seemed almost demonic to London's frightened population. Yet, to this day, despite numerous theories, we still have no idea who the mass murderer was.

> ***'I am down on whores and shant quit ripping them till I do get buckled.'***
>
> Jack the Ripper

Between 1888 and 1891, 11 young women were gruesomely murdered in the East End of London. The biggest problem in resolving these crimes is that experts simply cannot agree that one man committed all of the so-called Whitechapel Murders. A number of the victims had their throats cut and most suffered abdominal mutilation, but over the years the number of attacks blamed on the so-called Ripper changed as more was understood about the condition of the dead women and the nature of their injuries. Only five deaths are now confidently attributed to one killer – those of Mary Anne Nichols, Annie Chapman, Elizabeth Stride, Mary Kelly and Catherine Eddowes.

During the Whitechapel Murders, the East End lived in a state of terror. With no leads to go on, the police interviewed dozens of suspects, but all were released. Suspicion fell on local cranks and misfits, quack doctors, a barrister who committed suicide and even – but this was much later – a younger son of Queen Victoria. But there was never any hard evidence.

A Chilling Missive

In September 1888, the scandal reached new heights when the Central News Agency received a letter. Signed by 'Jack the Ripper', it said: 'I am down on

ABOVE: *MYTHS AND LEGENDS SURROUND THE MYSTERY OF THE WHITECHAPEL MURDERS.*

whores and shant quit ripping them till I do get buckled.' No evidence has ever been produced to suggest that the letter was genuine, but it captured the public imagination. The police were also sent part of a human liver with a note saying that the killer had enjoyed eating the other half after he'd cut it from one of his victims.

The murders continued and the story of Jack the Ripper appeared in newspapers all over the world. A myth arose that the murderer was a well-dressed gentleman who always carried a black bag; but this idea, like so many others, was simply a product of the hysteria that gripped the East End. Copycat letters were sent by the dozen to the police, as were more body parts, many of which were likely to have come from animals. In 1891, the murders came to an abrupt end, but the rumours about who – or what – was behind them have never entirely died down.

At the time it was seen as scandalous that the police could apparently do nothing to prevent such shocking murders in the greatest city in the world. The fact that the killer was never caught convinced people that there must be some kind of official cover up; that the killer was being protected because he was either well born or even a member of the Royal Family.

Prince Albert Victor, Duke of Clarence and grandson of Queen Victoria, was one suspect. He was known to frequent the Whitechapel area and on at least one occasion the Royal Family arranged to have an East End shopgirl institutionalized after the prince made her pregnant.

However, for all the suspicion and accusations, the mystery of Jack the Ripper remains unsolved to this day.

The Body in the Cellar
Dr Crippen

Perhaps the most horrific aspect of the murder of Cora Crippen by her husband Dr Peter Crippen (1862–1910) was not the murder itself – it was the way her body was treated after death. When the remains of Mrs Crippen were discovered under the floor of the coal cellar in the couple's Camden Town house in July 1910, the police found a body that had been filleted. Her flesh was there, but her skull and skeleton had been neatly removed and were never found.

The murder of Mrs Crippen would probably have remained undetected were it not for the concerns of John and Lillian Nash, who went to Scotland Yard in June 1910 to report that their friend Cora had disappeared without trace in February. The couple had become suspicious because, earlier that year, they'd met Dr Crippen at a ball where, rather than being accompanied by his wife, he was accompanied by his secretary, Ethel Le Neve. On its own this might not have aroused the Nashs' suspicions, but they

RIGHT: WHEN ETHEL LE NEVE STARTED WEARING CORA CRIPPEN'S JEWELLERY, FRIENDS BECAME SUSPICIOUS.

noticed that Ethel was wearing Mrs Crippen's jewellery.

Soon after that incident the Nashs left for a holiday in America. When they returned to England they visited Dr Crippen and asked about Cora. Crippen claimed that Cora had died while on a trip to America, although, bizarrely, he couldn't remember exactly where in America this had happened!

The detective assigned to the case agreed with Mr and Mrs Nash that something was amiss. In July 1910, Chief Inspector Walter Drew visited Crippen. When asked about his wife, the doctor immediately changed his story and claimed that he'd invented her death because he was too embarrassed to admit that she'd run off with another man. Drew and his accompanying officers searched the house, but found nothing suspicious and left saying they would return the next day to sort out a few minor reports and other details.

Manhunt

This is where Crippen made the mistake that was to cost him his life. He packed his things and fled his home. When the police returned to the house the next day they discovered that both Crippen and Ethel Le Neve had vanished. It was as good as an admission of guilt.

An international manhunt began and, even without the benefit of modern communications, the net quickly closed on the runaway couple. The captain of a ship bound for Canada had noticed an odd couple aboard, and when he saw the newspaper stories about the suspects he put two and two together. He sent a message by telegraph saying that he was convinced he had the fugitives on board. Crippen had shaved his moustache off and was growing a beard, while the 'young man' who accompanied him was 'undoubtedly a girl'. Chief Inspector Drew boarded another ship and immediately set off in pursuit of the pair. Crippen and Le Neve were arrested before they could land at Montreal and were returned to Britain for trial. The story was one of the newspaper sensations of the age. Crippen was hanged at Pentonville Prison in November 1910. Ethel Le Neve was cleared of all guilt – and then she vanished.

The World's Greatest Swindler
Horatio William Bottomley

Horatio William Bottomley (1860–1933) was an MP, newspaper publisher, journalist and orator, and probably the most outrageous swindler of all time. He cheated thousands of individuals, institutions, the City and even the government of which he was a member.

Born in Hackney in poverty, Bottomley spent his childhood in an orphanage. He left school at 14 and became a solicitor's clerk, which gave him the grounding to achieve wealth and power. Bottomley subsequently bought an ailing newspaper and a couple of small printing firms and formed a company that began to make money. But, in spite of the company's wealth, he could not resist milking it dry. He spent millions of invested money on extravagant schemes – horses, travel, country houses and flats in various towns. The company eventually crashed and he ended up in the High Court on a charge of fraud. During his trial, he spent much of the time correcting the judge on points of law, tied the prosecution up in knots and convinced judge, jury, and public that he was a victimized underdog. He escaped with a warning.

Kippers and Champagne

Bottomley continued on his triumphant way, always insisting on kippers and champagne for breakfast and keeping a string of mistresses in London and the provinces. Without bothering to learn about horses, he nonetheless bought, sold and raced them with complete and reckless abandon. In ten years he spent an estimated £23 million of other people's money, and his personal success was crowned when he was elected Liberal MP for Hackney in 1905. As part of his election campaign he saddled all his racehorses and sent them down Hackney High Street with 'vote for my owner' emblazoned on their saddles. He ran a sweepstake on the 1914 Derby in one of his papers, which was won by a 'little old lady' living near Toulouse. A suspicious journalist discovered that the 'little old lady' was actually Bottomley himself.

Finally, he cheated an associate who told all to the courts. Bottomley was tried in 1922, during which he produced another brilliant speech, concluding with the declaration that it would be the most appalling miscarriage of justice if he was found guilty. But his silver tongue was not enough to save him this time and he was sentenced to seven years' penal servitude. While sewing mailbags a visitor saw him at work and said, 'Sewing, I see'. 'No, reaping,' he replied. He was released and died penniless in 1933.

The Acid Bath Murderer
John Haigh

John Haigh, the notorious 'Acid Bath Murderer', is proof that a strict religious upbringing isn't always all that it's cut out to be. Haigh's father, a devout Christian, never allowed his son to play with or meet other children, constantly telling him 'It will not please the Lord'. The extent to which Haigh's childhood damaged him will never be known, but one thing we do know is that he grew up to become one of the worst serial killers of the 20th century. He seems to have killed because it gave him a sense of power and control. None of his victims was particularly wealthy – in fact, the most Haigh obtained from the majority of them was the use of their ration-books. Society would have been far less obsessed with the murders if they had been committed for money – it was the fact that they seemed so inexplicable that made them so terrifying.

Haigh appeared to be the least likely serial killer when police first inter-viewed him. He was well-educated, charming and much liked by his Kensington neighbours, but gradually the police uncovered the shocking truth about his victims. The murder – one of at least six – that led to his conviction was that of a 69-year-old widow named Olive Durand-Deacon. Haigh befriended her and offered her help when she asked his advice about marketing cosmetics. He invited her to his factory in Crawley, Sussex. Haigh led her into what he called his 'workshop', stepped up behind her and shot her in the back of the neck. He then put the body into a large drum of sulphuric acid and went home. Two days later he returned to make sure the body had dissolved – it had turned into a brown sludge.

Haigh was convinced he could kill as often as he liked without the risk of capture, as he believed that without a body there could be no conviction. What

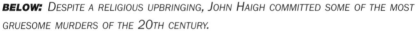

BELOW: *Despite a religious upbringing, John Haigh committed some of the most gruesome murders of the 20th century.*

he didn't know was that acid does not dissolve everything. The police later found spots of blood and a plastic denture that was identified as belonging to Mrs Durand-Deacon.

Caught Out

When he was arrested, Haigh continued to insist that he could not be tried as there was no body. When the police amassed enough evidence to bring the case to court, he came up with a second line of defence. He told the court that, having shot each victim, he cut through an artery and drank their blood before placing the body in a bath of acid. He claimed that he had to consume human blood, as he was a vampire. The prosecution countered that this was a ruse and Haigh was trying to escape a guilty verdict on the grounds of insanity. The plea failed and the police evidence – including the victims' ration-books, which were found at his home – led to a guilty verdict.

The newspapers had been filled with sensational stories about Haigh in the weeks leading up to and including the trial, but the mystery of his real motivation, if there ever was one, for the crimes went to the grave with him after he was hanged at Wandsworth prison in August 1949.

The Heist of the Century
The Great Train Robbery

The Great Train Robbery of 1963 was one of the most audacious crimes in history, netting the 13-man gang that committed the crime over £2,000,000 – easily the equivalent of £40,000,000 in today's money. But it wasn't just the amount of money stolen that made the robbery one of the most scandalous in history – it was the extraordinarily long sentences that were handed down when the gang was eventually tried and convicted. As one commentator pointed out: 'If you murdered a man in cold blood you'd have got half the sentence the train robbers got.'

Brains and Brawn

The gang that committed the Great Train Robbery was a curious mix of brains and brawn. The mastermind was Bruce Reynolds, an antiques dealer with expensive tastes who had inside information about mail trains that carried cash and valuables. Buster Edwards and Gordon Goody provided the muscle, while John Wheater, a solicitor, provided a respectable front as well as a remote Oxfordshire farmhouse where the gang intended to lie low after the robbery. Ronnie Biggs, the youngest member of the gang and the one who became famous for his part in the heist, was there because he had a friend (who was never caught) who could drive the train after it had been taken over.

The planning of the crime was meticulous. The robbery had to take place at night and on a stretch of track close enough to London to avoid long absences by any member of the gang, as most of them were known in the London criminal underworld. If any or all of them disappeared completely it would immediately arouse suspicion. The gang bought blue railway workers' uniforms and a fake set of red lights with which to stop the train.

At 3am on 8 August 1963, the train came to a halt at the fake red light. The train's fireman climbed down from the cab to see what was going on and was immediately taken down the embankment by one of the gang. He put up no resistance. The driver, Jack Mills, walked back through the train to see what was going on, was coshed and never recovered from his injuries.

A hitch occurred when the gang's driver was unable to move the train, so the injured driver was forced to do it. The train was driven to a position a few hundred yards up the track, the mail coach was broken into and 120 sacks of mail were transferred to a waiting van.

The Getaway

The gang retreated to the farmhouse at Leatherslade in Oxfordshire. Within days they became aware that the police were tracking them down and they made a run for it. Their mistake was to leave fingerprints all over the house. The 13 robbers managed, however, to leave Britain and hole up in various countries, but all were eventually brought back. Buster Edwards returned voluntarily from Mexico after three years. The gang was tried and sentenced. Ronnie Biggs, probably the least important member of the gang, came to symbolize the heist of the century, as the robbery was known, because he escaped from Wandsworth Prison just 15 months into his sentence. He fled to Brazil where he was to live for more than 30 years before returning to the UK – and prison – in 2001.

The Great Train Robbery exposed the complete lack of security around those responsible for moving large amounts of money around the country. The Establishment was also determined to impose harsh sentences on the gang – a total of 300 years between them all, in fact – because the amount of money involved was so great. It is true that the injuries sustained by the train driver, Jack Mills, were a factor, but the judge's real concern was to show that spectacular crimes would receive spectacular sentences.

'If you murdered a man in cold blood you'd have got half the sentence the train robbers got.'

The Aristocratic Murderer

Lord Lucan

When Lord Lucan murdered his children's nanny some 30 years ago a scandal began that resonates to this day. After the killing, which occurred in London's swanky Belgravia, Lucan drove to the south coast and vanished. For years, sightings of the disgraced peer were reported in various parts of the world, but none was confirmed. If Lucan is still alive – and this must be seriously doubted – he is unlikely ever to be found.

The murder was committed on the night of 7 November, 1974. It didn't just expose the life of the Lucans to the public gaze, it also led to endless newspaper stories about the louche lifestyle of a group of very right-wing ex-public schoolboys who were even accused of plotting against Harold Wilson's Labour government.

The sordid tale began just before 10pm on that gloomy November night, when a slight woman, clearly distraught and covered in blood, ran screaming into the Plumber's Arms in Lower Belgrave Street, a road in the heart of one of London's most exclusive districts. The woman was almost incoherent with terror, but witnesses said later that they made out the following words: 'I've just escaped from being murdered. He's in the house. He's murdered the nanny!'

Within minutes the police had arrived at the pub and the woman was identified as Lady Lucan. When the police searched the Lucans' home, 46 Lower Belgrave Street, they found the couple's three children unharmed and asleep in bed. But downstairs a grim sight awaited them – the floor and walls of the breakfast room were covered in blood, and in a blood-soaked sack near the entrance to the kitchen they found the body of Sandra Rivett, the nanny. Nearby was a short length of lead piping, which was later identified as the weapon that killed the young woman. A murder hunt began and the police quickly established the sequence of events after the murder had taken place.

A friend and neighbour of the Lucans, Mrs Madeleine Floorman, heard her doorbell ring soon after 10pm, but assuming it was youngsters fooling around she ignored it. Then her phone rang. The caller was almost incoherent, but Mrs Floorman later said she was sure it was Lord Lucan, a judgment that seemed to be confirmed by the presence of some minute spots of blood, which were later discovered on her front doorstep.

At 10.30pm Lucan phoned his mother in north London and asked her to pick up the children. She immediately headed south from her house in St John's Wood and found her daughter-in-law's house filled with police. She took the children with her having given the police her son's address – the Lucans were separated. The police found his flat empty and his car still outside.

It was quickly established that Lucan had driven a borrowed car to Uckfield in Sussex, where he arrived at the home of his friends Ian and Susan Maxwell-Scott at about 11.30pm. Mrs Maxwell-Scott later told police that Lucan was dishevelled and his trousers were wet, as if he had attempted to clean them.

Lucan's Version

Though clearly upset, Lucan had told Mrs Maxwell-Scott his version of events. He claimed that while walking past his wife's house he'd looked in through a window and seen Lady Lucan struggling with an intruder. He rushed into the house – he still had a key – but slipped and fell in a pool of blood before he could reach his wife and her assailant. By the time he'd picked himself up the intruder had gone. He took Lady Lucan to the bathroom, but while they were there she slipped past him and ran into the street. He then panicked and ran off.

Lucan left his friends' house and a little after midnight rang his mother again, probably from a phone box. He then wrote two letters, both of which were addressed to Bill Shand Kydd, who was married to his sister. One letter said that he knew he would have no chance in a court of law and wished to spare his children the sight of their father accused of murder. The other related to his financial affairs. Lucan left the Maxwell-Scotts saying he had to 'get back', but his car was later found at Newhaven. It contained significant amounts of blood, which was later identified to be of the same blood type as that of the dead nanny.

An Upper-class Life

In an earlier age Lord Lucan might have been less harshly judged. Being unemployed and unemployable – and he was both of these – were once seen as the great defining virtues of the well bred. Gentlemen like Lucan simply didn't work, as it was beneath them. Lucan was also supremely arrogant and absolutely convinced of his own abilities. He'd launched his career as a professional gambler on the basis of one lucky win and it was a career that brought him to the verge of financial ruin – by the time he murdered Sandra Rivett he was virtually bankrupt.

Lucan also appears to have been involved with a group of very right-wing friends who believed that Britain was going to the dogs and that it could only be saved by well-born aristocrats like themselves. Sadly, Lucan lived in an age in which being born into an aristocratic family was simply not enough, and many of Lucan's problems stemmed from a belief that his 'well-bred' qualities would open the doors to power. After a

'I've just escaped from being murdered. He's in the house. He's murdered the nanny!'

Lady Lucan

ABOVE: *LORD LUCAN DISAPPEARED MYSTERIOUSLY AFTER THE BRUTAL MURDER OF HIS CHILDREN'S NANNY AND A VIOLENT ATTACK ON HIS WIFE.*

career in the Army and a short spell at a merchant bank, his gambling career had failed him – his belief in his abilities was never matched by the reality of his increasing losses at the gaming tables.

Lucan had married Veronica Duncan in 1964, and thereafter spent his nights gambling and his days asleep and dining at his club The couple had three children, two girls and a boy, but their marriage came under enormous stress, as Lady Lucan was concerned about her husband's massive financial losses. They separated in 1972 and a custody battle ensued with Lucan attempting to turn his wife's history of post-natal depression into a full-blown psychiatric disorder that would increase his chances of getting the children.

Lucan was also convinced that as a peer of the realm the courts would naturally favour his claim, but times had changed and the children were returned to their mother. There began a bizarre period during which Lucan spied on his wife and children – or paid others to do so – making secret tape recordings and discussing the possibility of bribing his wife to go away. All the time his debts grew. We know, too, that Lucan discussed the possibility of murdering his wife – his motive being to get possession of the house and thereby stave off bankruptcy.

Different Theories

Whatever else happened on the night of the murder itself, there is no doubt that Lady Lucan was badly injured – a doctor recorded lacerations on her scalp and severe bruising to her throat and in her mouth. At an inquest into the death of Sandra Rivett, the jury recorded a verdict of 'murder by Lord Lucan'.

Some still believe that Lord Lucan was innocent and that he really did disturb the real murderer who has never been caught. Another theory is that Lucan arrived at the house knowing that a murderer he had hired would have killed his wife. He then had to dispose of the body, but it all went wrong when Lucan discovered that the hit man had killed the nanny, who was similar in height to Lady Lucan, instead. This left Lord Lucan no option but to kill his wife himself.

Lady Lucan did not think her husband had hired a hit man to kill her but, although it seems unlikely that Lord Lucan would mistake his wife for the nanny, it was dark in the house at the time of the attack. Also, Lord Lucan would have been in a state of enormous tension. Particularly damning for Lucan was the bloodstained lead pipe – part was found in the house and part in the car he abandoned at Newhaven. His wife later testified that the man who hit her and then told her to shut up was indeed her husband. Certainly, it is difficult to believe that a professional hit man would have used a messy, inefficient lead cosh to kill.

Lucan said he had found his wife covered in blood in the breakfast room – yet there were no splashes of her blood in this room, only at the head of the stairs, precisely where she claimed she had been attacked.

Other parts of Lucan's story collapsed under examination: there were no signs of anyone slipping and falling in blood in the house, for example, only of someone stepping in blood.

All the evidence suggests that Lord Lucan was indeed the murderer and, the fact that he vanished – and probably jumped from a cross-channel ferry on the journey to France – did not save the family honour, which is certainly what Lucan had hoped. When he came of age, his son, the 8th Lord Lucan, decided never to use the title.

Brinks-Matt Bullion
Robbery at Heathrow

The theft of more than £26,000,000 in gold bullion from a Heathrow warehouse in November 1983 exposed the scandalously lax airport security at one of the world's busiest airports. It was also the biggest robbery ever seen in the United Kingdom at the time and was certainly one of the most audacious. The police were initially baffled, and to this day much of the money has not been recovered, despite the eventual prosecution of most of the men involved.

South London gangster Kenneth Noye, later jailed for murder in a separate case, is believed to have been involved in the crime, along with Michael McAvoy and Brian Robinson who were both jailed for 25 years. The meticulously planned robbery, which was carried out on a quiet weekend, relied entirely on inside information – a guard at the Brinks-Matt warehouse had been persuaded to tell the gang when the bullion would be there and help them gain entry. However, he was the weak link that led to the arrests.

On the day of the robbery, the guard was tied up so that it seemed as if he'd been a victim of the robbers, but by all accounts he wasn't a good enough actor to fool the police and he eventually broke down during questioning. By then, the 6,800 stolen gold ingots had been converted into untraceable cash.

The police were hugely embarrassed by the robbery, and such was the scandal surrounding it that police practices in London aimed at targeting career criminals were completely overhauled.

Maxwell's Millions
Robert Maxwell

The scandal of Robert Maxwell (1923–91) – or the Bouncing Czech as the satirical magazine *Private Eye* memorably called him – was that he was able to bully so many people who should have known better into thinking that he was one of the good guys. Eminent politicians, journalists, businessmen and financial regulators were steamrollered or cajoled into accepting some of the dodgiest financial practices in business history. It was only when the 20-stone crook fell from his yacht and drowned that the full story of his corrupt business empire came to light.

Born Jan Ludvig Koch in Czechoslovakia, Maxwell lost his parents during the Holocaust, but managed to reach Britain in 1940. He served in the Army where he was commended for bravery. After the Second World War, he set up a successful company that published scientific journals. By the 1960s, Maxwell had established the highly profitable Pergamon Press. However, an enquiry by the Department of Trade and Industry (DTI) following an American bid to take over Pergamon in 1969 concluded that he was not fit to run a publicly quoted company.

Undaunted, Maxwell took over the British Printing Corporation in 1980 and renamed it Maxwell Communications. He bought Mirror Newspapers in 1984, by which time his financial empire stretched across the globe. Only Maxwell was aware that his empire was slipping into debt. The purchase of an American publisher only made things worse and even the flotation of Mirror Group Newspapers in 1991 could do little to save him.

Man Overboard

No one has solved the mystery of Maxwell's death – did he fall, jump or was he pushed? Whatever the answer, this sudden end meant that Maxwell escaped justice. Within a few days of his demise, and without his giant bullying presence, the extent of his company's debts became apparent. The biggest scandal of his financial career, however, was revealed when it was discovered that he had stolen millions of pounds from his company's pension funds in a desperate attempt to stave off bankruptcy.

A sale of Maxwell's personal effects at Sotheby's revealed the extent of his greed – piles of hotel towels and dressing gowns that he'd stolen from hotels were included in the sale. But the extent of his influence over otherwise sane people can be judged by the fact that a senior journalist, then working on Maxwell's newspaper the *Daily Mirror*, punched a *Guardian* journalist who'd dared to suggest that Maxwell's death was no great loss.

Maxwell's sons, Ian and Kevin, were tried and acquitted on charges of defrauding Mirror Group pensions. A DTI report blamed Maxwell alone for the collapse of his financial empire, and legal action against auditors led to a huge out of court settlement that largely compensated the pensioners Maxwell had robbed. The government also had to pay out £100,000,000 in compensation.

Guinness Gold
Ernest Saunders

A scandal that reverberated for years, led to the trial and conviction of some of the biggest names in the financial world of the mid-1980s and resulted in changes in the law was the Guinness share-price fiasco. The story began when a company called Argyll (now Safeway) made a takeover bid for Distillers. Ernest Saunders, the chief executive of the brewing firm Guinness, launched a counter bid. However, in order to find the money for this, he and his fellow directors had to organize a share issue, and to make this attractive to potential buyers they also had to ensure that the price of existing shares did not fall.

To eliminate any risk, Saunders and a number of other senior Guinness executives secretly told a group of businessmen that if they bought Guinness shares they would not lose out whatever happened. In some cases, Guinness even paid these individuals from its own coffers so they would have the money to buy large quantities of the new shares. It was insider trading of the worst sort, because genuine share buyers believed that the share price reflected the true state of the company which, of course, it did not. Ernest Saunders, Jack Lyons, Anthony Parnes and Gerald Ronson were the ringleaders of what was really a share price-fixing scam.

In 1990, the four men were put on trial for fraud – three were imprisoned but Lyons escaped on the grounds of ill health and Saunders was released from jail early on similar grounds. Saunders' doctors said he had Alzheimer's Disease, but when he was released he miraculously recovered and, as a number of satirical commentators pointed out, he is believed to be the only person ever to recover from what is normally a degenerative illness that leads inevitably to death.

In the years that followed their conviction, the four men made repeated attempts to have their convictions overturned – each failed, which goes to show that there are some cases, although not many, where wealth can't buy you the thing you really want.

LEFT: *ERNEST SAUNDERS AND HIS FAMILY ON TRIAL DAY.*

The Collapse of the World's Oldest Bank

Nick Leeson

Barings, the world's oldest bank, was founded in 1762. By the late 20th century it was still being run by gentlemen for gentlemen – which really meant that those in control were too grand to do any of the day-to-day banking work. However, they were happy to reap the profits, while they, so it was said, spent much of their time lunching at their clubs while clever comprehensive-educated boys did the dirty work on the trading floor. Nick Leeson, whose background was nothing like that of his public school-educated masters, was the bank's star trader on the Singapore Derivatives market. But, as Leeson climbed up the ranks, he gradually lost touch with the real world – a situation that was exacerbated by pressure from his bosses to make increasing amounts of money.

As Chief Trader, Leeson was in charge of trading and he was also in charge of settlements. This meant that he did the deals, but also settled the accounts of what had been bought and sold at the end of each day. When he began to make losses instead of profits, he transferred them to a secret account numbered 88888. He convinced his gentlemanly bosses in London that he needed more cash on the grounds that it was to cover client trading. In fact, Leeson was trading with the bank's money and also using it to cover his losses. He must have believed that a lucky break – a spectacularly successful deal – would rescue him from the vastly increasing losses that were concealed in account 88888 – but it was not to be.

An earthquake in Japan caused a stock market crash and Barings' losses, which jumped from bad to astronomically bad, could no longer be concealed. In February 1995, Leeson fled the country and was eventually arrested in Germany from where he was extradited to Singapore. He was tried and sentenced to six-and-a-half years in prison. He served about half his sentence before being released. Barings itself collapsed as a result of Leeson's activities and its gentlemanly directors found they were out of a job – the days when bosses allowed their employees the sort of freedom enjoyed by Leeson were over. Leeson's final unauthorized losses totalled a sum in the region of £800,000,000

Barings' auditors were successfully sued by their liquidators for failing in their duty as a financial institution and the scandal sent shock waves through the financial markets of the world that are still felt today. In 1998, *Rogue Trader*, a film based on Leeson's autobiography, was released.

> *'I was always working in the best interests of the bank.'*
>
> Nick Leeson

The Bank of Criminals and Conmen International
Bringing Down BCCI

When the Bank of Credit and Commerce International (BCCI) collapsed owing some £10 billion, two huge financial scandals emerged. The first was that an international bank could get into such a mess – a mess that caused huge suffering to tens of thousands of trusting customers. The second was that the Bank of England, which should have regulated the running of BCCI, ended up on trial on charges of neglect and incompetence brought by the liquidators of BCCI.

BCCI started life in 1972. It was founded and funded by Pakistani millionaire, Agha Hasan Abedi, and grew rapidly until it had more than 14,000 employees and offices in 70 countries. Throughout its history there were warnings that it accepted money from corrupt governments, dictatorships and arms and drug dealers. But the truth was hard to find, precisely because Abedi refused to talk. It may well have suited the governments of a number of countries, including Britain, to have at its beck and call a bank that was so shrouded in secrecy that covert operations could be run and funded through its finances. These were some of the allegations that emerged after the bank's collapse.

The real problems began in the late 1970s when one of the bank's biggest borrowers – the Gulf Shipping Group – was about to file for bankruptcy. Abedi and others were terrified they too would be dragged down so they began to falsify the books – depositors' accounts were robbed to pay for investments that made it look as it the bank was trading normally and fictitious accounts and transactions were created.

The action against the Bank of England was brought by the liquidators who had been hired to sort out the mess when BCCI collapsed. In court, counsel accused Bank of England officials of being afraid of BCCI and the dangers it posed. Counsel also accused Bank of England officials of bending the rules to suit BCCI, despite evidence from a number of individuals that the man who ran and dominated BCCI, Abedi, was corrupt. All the warning signs were there, the court heard, but they were ignored. Even senior Bank of England officials had described BCCI as a disaster waiting to happen. Abedi was described as resembling Charles Dickens's Uriah Heep, craven yet hugely manipulative. It was argued that when a conflict of interest arose between investors and the bank itself, the latter was always given priority. One of the saddest ironies about BCCI is that many British Muslims transferred their money into the bank precisely because it was run by Muslims.

Mr Abedi, it transpired in court, had set up and run BCCI specifically to avoid the risk of prying from the regulators. Even the Bank of America had warned that BCCI's business practices were far from satisfactory, yet nothing was done. The Bank of England, it seems, was the only institution that did not realize that, long before its demise, BCCI was popularly known as the Bank of Criminals and Conmen International.

Spies and Secrecy

But the real scandal of BCCI went much further. Long after BCCI officials had been jailed, the British Government refused to allow any investigation into the bank, largely, it was believed, because MI6 had been among those who had used the highly secretive BCCI to transfer payments for dodgy operations around the world. However, the government was finally forced to open an investigation into the bank's dealings in 1992.

The official enquiry that the British Government had done so much to prevent castigated the Bank of England for its failures, but it was only 12 years later that the case against the institution came to be tested in court. It seemed then that the bank officials' only defence was that they had presided over a cock-up rather than deliberately avoiding their duty to regulate BCCI. As this book went to press, the case against the Bank of England – the first of its kind in history – continued. If the case is upheld, the bank will have to find almost £1 billion, together with legal fees that have run into tens of millions.

Clerics with Red Faces
– Irreverent Reverends and Vice-Ridden Vicars

'In restoring man from evil sovereignty, we must cheat.'
The Reverend Moon

The Man who'd Marry Anyone
Reverend Alexander Keith

Until the end of the 19th century, one of London's strangest churches stood opposite Crew House in Curzon Street. The Mayfair Chapel was, until the Marriage Act of 1754, a continual thorn in the side of the authorities, as it was here that the eccentric clergyman, Reverend Alexander Keith, conducted marriage ceremonies for anyone who turned up, at any time of day or night, with absolutely no questions asked.

For young runaways and the romantically inclined in an age when marriage was largely a matter of convenience, financial or otherwise, the Mayfair Chapel was a godsend. The authorities and the Establishment hated it because it represented a threat to the financial and dynastic plans they had for their offspring, but Alexander Keith knew the law and he was perfectly entitled to do what he was doing.

The popularity of the Mayfair Chapel can be judged by the fact that in just one year – 1742 – Keith married no fewer than 700 couples – and all with neither licence nor banns. Parliament made several attempts to change the law to make these marriages illegal, but they immediately abandoned the attempt when they realized – particularly those in the House of Lords – that to do so would be to render many of their own grandchildren illegitimate. The potential scandal was too great to be borne.

Among the most famous marriages conducted at the Mayfair chapel was that between the Duke of Hamilton and Elizabeth Dunning, one of the great beauties of Georgian England. The couple were in such a hurry that an old brass washer had to be used in place of a gold band!

The World's Most Absent-minded Man
George Harvest

Educated at Oxford University, the first choice of career for George Harvest (1728–89) was acting. However, this was unsuccessful and he instead took holy orders. Harvest also decided to get married, but he was so forgetful that when the great day dawned he went fishing, not returning until nightfall. Only then did he remember that he should have been at the village church.

Harvest's life as a clergyman was filled with outrages – so much so that he came close to being defrocked on a number of occasions. He was the parish priest of Thames Ditton in Surrey for more than 30 years, and in that time he turned absent-mindedness into an art form. However, despite his extraordinary forgetfulness – which infuriated his superiors – he was a good-hearted man and much liked by his congregation, which probably explains how he managed to keep his job for so long.

When Harvest wrote a letter he often wrote it to one person, addressed it to another and posted it to a third. Paying a visit to London he passed a beggar in the street. The beggar raised his hat in hopes of being given a penny, but Harvest was in such a dream that he merely thought it was an acquaintance and raised his hat in return. The list of his forgetful escapades is legion.

When he needed to travel, Harvest almost always had to borrow a horse, for he usually mislaid his own after a few days. He had a terrible tendency to lose those he borrowed too, and eventually no one would lend him a horse no matter how dire the emergency.

Other stories of his strange behaviour include his frequent attempts to leave friends' houses by going upstairs instead of down, and getting lost on the way home. He often went into a neighbour's house at night thinking it was his own, and would later be found fast asleep in the wrong bed.

Not Once, but Twice

Towards the end of his life he made a second marriage proposal and was accepted. On the day of the wedding he woke early, and finding the weather glorious he wandered off to Richmond, where he met some friends and passed a delightful day without so much as a glimmer of memory that his bride-to-be and her family were waiting for him some miles off.

On another occasion, he managed to become separated from his friends on a trip to Calais. He spoke no French, but he was keen to return to his hotel, which was called the Silver Lion. So he 'put a silver shilling in his mouth and set himself in the attitude of a lion rampant… and after exciting much admiration was led back to the inn by a soldier who thought he was a maniac escaped from his keepers'.

His bizarre actions in public included a visit to a London theatre during which his old and very grubby night-cap fell from his head and into the theatre pit, where it was thrown backwards and forwards by the audience. Afraid it would never be returned to him, Harvest stood up in the middle of the play and preached for ten minutes, concluding that 'it is a very serious thing to die without a nightcap'. To which he added 'I shall be restless tonight if I have not my cap'. Obviously, the audience were struck by his manner, because the cap was handed back up to him on the end of a stick.

At a grand dinner with Lady Onslow and a number of distinguished guests Harvest spotted a large fly on his neighbour's bonnet. He leapt to his feet and shouted 'May you be married!' at the top of his voice and struck the woman a violent blow on the head. In fact, he hit her so hard he knocked her out.

Needless to say, Lady Onslow did not invite him to dinner again.

In the Victorian era, Harvest would have quickly lost his job, but before then the Church protected its own, whatever they got up to – short of murder. Harvest was forgetful to the point of negligence throughout his adult life, but that was just something his parishioners and colleagues had to suffer.

The Leap-frogging Bishop of Derry
Frederick Hervey, Earl of Bristol

Frederick Hervey (1730–1803) studied at Westminster School and Cambridge University. Through the influence of his brother, the 3rd Earl of Bristol, Hervey was made Bishop of Cloyne in 1767, although, as he himself admitted, he had absolutely no connection with or interest in Ireland. However, he soon started manoeuvring for the bishopric of Derry, which was worth more money than that of Cloyne. Again aided by his brother, Hervey was given the job in 1768. When he heard the news he was playing leapfrog with his fellow clergy in the garden at Cloyne Palace and is reported to have shouted: 'I will jump no more, gentlemen. I have surpassed you all, and jumped from Cloyne to Derry!'

Hervey was 39, married, and earning a reputation as an eccentric, largely because he was sympathetic to the local Catholic population which, under English rule, could own virtually nothing nor hold any office of any worth. His outspoken views on the subject almost led to his impeachment for treason, and many English parliamentarians, including Robert Walpole and Charles James Fox, thought him 'a scandal to the Church and the nation'.

Bishop Bristol

Hervey got nowhere with his radical views, however, and instead developed his eccentric personality and ability to shock. He built three huge houses, his favourite, perched on a clifftop at Lough Foyle, was the size of Blenheim Palace in Oxfordshire. On the death of his brother in 1778, he became the 4th Earl of Bristol and earned the nickname 'Bishop Bristol'. His house parties were legendary; he often invited the fattest members of the clergy to stay and made them race against each other. If he invited the wives of the clergy along too, he sprinkled flour outside their bedroom doors to see if he could catch them moving about during the night.

Hervey became a byword for irreverence, and the authorities were so

OPPOSITE: *Frederick Hervey, Bishop of Derry, made fat clergymen run races against each other.*

convinced that he would bring disgrace on the Church that they considered trying to get rid of him – but he was simply too powerful.

In his latter years, Hervey travelled extensively in France and Italy, and spent so lavishly that many hotels bear the name 'Bristol' to this day. His cook always rode on ahead of his carriage so that his food was ready when he arrived at the next inn. After a while, he received a petition criticizing him for being absent from his parish for so long. However, he sent each signatory an inflated pig's bladder containing a dried pea along with a copy of the following verse:

> *Three large bluebottles sat upon three bladders.*
> *Blow bottle flies, blow; burst, blow bladder burst*
> *A new-blown bladder and three blue balls make a great rattle.*
> *So rattle bladder rattle.*

What more can one say?

> ### *'I will jump no more, gentlemen. I have surpassed you all, and jumped from Cloyne to Derry!'*
>
> Frederick Hervey, Bishop of Derry

Mr Wroe's Virgins
John Wroe

The scandalous story of Mr Wroe's virgins really begins with a woman called Joanna Southcott (1750–1814). Born in Ottery St Mary, Devon, Southcott grew up claiming she had the gift of prophecy. However, she declined to give much detail about her prophecies, but said she had sealed them in a special box that was not to be opened until some time in the future – she didn't specify when.

Somehow, she attracted a growing band of followers and Southcottian societies, which believed that Christ's second coming was imminent, sprang up all over England and spread as far as America. In the year of her death, Southcott claimed that she would bear the next Messiah. Needless to say she didn't, as by then she was in her mid-60s, but it was at about this time that John Wroe (1782–1863), the son of a Bradford cloth-maker, joined a Southcottian society. He was said to have had regular visions as a child and was keen to point this out to his new companions.

Wroe visited Ashton-under-Lyme to meet its Southcottians and discovered that they had a number of wealthy patrons. He began to dominate the Ashton society and was baptized in a local river. He then began to issue orders, including a decree that all male Southcottians should be circumcised and that only kosher meat should be eaten. Wroe planned to enclose the whole town within a wall, and although this never happened he persuaded local people to part with a small fortune to build a temple.

His followers wore white robes and were forbidden to shave or cut their hair, but as Wroe's grip on the cult tightened he began to demand more and more. He persuaded his followers to build him a mansion and then announced that God had told him he should always be accompanied by seven virgins. Unfortunately, at least two of these 'virgins' quickly became pregnant and Wroe had to leave Ashton in disgrace. Such was the outrage that the whole town rioted.

The Southcottian society lived on in Ashton, but with much reduced numbers. Wroe seems to have been sufficiently rehabilitated to receive £2,000 to publish Joanna Southcott's prophecies – he spent the money building himself a house. Eventually – pursued, no doubt, by numerous creditors and angry Southcottians – Wroe left England for Australia where he died. Amazingly, given the scandal surrounding Wroe's behaviour, remnants of the society he dominated survive to this day in several countries.

A Craze for Fallen Women
Reverend Harold Davidson

As recent scandals involving the Church have shown, it's very difficult for a clergyman to be defrocked. A priest or a vicar has to be extremely badly behaved indeed for the Church to do anything about his bad behaviour as the Church

RIGHT: *PROSTITUTES TESTIFIED AGAINST REVEREND HAROLD DAVIDSON.*

protects its own. But there is a limit and one Norfolk vicar went beyond it in the 1920s and 1930s and paid the price.

The clergyman in question was the Reverend Harold Davidson of Stiffkey (pronounced Stewkey). Davidson regularly visited London, where he loitered around Piccadilly Circus, approached prostitutes and attempted, he claimed, to rescue them. Suspicions were aroused when it transpired that his interest centred on saving young, attractive prostitutes – preferably between the ages of 14 and 20!

Such was the respect afforded to a man of the cloth back in the 1920s that Davidson got away with his behaviour for a long time – he was vicar from 1906 to 1932. By 1930, he was spending most of the week in London. But even on Sundays, when he was in Norfolk to minister to his parishioners, his behaviour was decidedly eccentric. He regularly cycled into the church on his bicycle, leaping off to begin the service when he reached the altar. Things came to a head in 1931, when he failed to turn up for a commemorative service on Armistice Day.

The churchwarden was furious when Davidson failed to take the Armistice service and reported the incident to the Bishop of Norwich. Thus began the most scandalous ecclesiastical trial in history. Prostitutes were brought from London to testify, and although some supported the vicar, others accused him of having a sexual interest in them. Davidson denied all the charges, professing his innocence to the last. But the prosecution dropped a bombshell, as they had a photograph of Davidson in a compromising position – standing next to a naked girl and apparently taking more than a platonic interest in her bottom. The vicar was duly defrocked.

The Performing Vicar

Undaunted, Davidson took acting lessons and launched a theatrical career, cashing in on the fame his trial had brought him. He went to Blackpool, where he sat in a barrel surrounded by posters accusing the Church of various outrages. The crowds who come to see him eventually became so unmanageable that there was a risk of riot and the police were called in. He travelled the country, sometimes accompanied by a dead whale or caged lions. His patter always centred on the perfidy of the Church and many of his performances showed how badly he felt he'd been treated. During one show he was chained up while several dwarves danced around him sticking forks in his bottom as if he was in hell – sent there quite unfairly of course by his persecutors in the Church.

He died in 1938 – no-one seems quite sure when he was born – after a performance in the lions' cage went wrong and he was badly mauled – but his love of publicity never left him and legend has it that his last words were: 'Don't miss the evening edition!'.

ABOVE: *William Hogarth produced a series of engravings in the 18th century satirizing the vices of both high and low life in England. This engraving, entitled 'Gin Lane', illustrated the impact of hard liquor on London society.*

ABOVE: *London's Haymarket area, just south of Piccadilly Circus, was a popular place for prostitutes to offer their services to well-to-do gentlemen in the 19th century.*

ABOVE: *Showgirl* Christine Keeler *was a key player in the* Profumo Affair, *a sex and politics scandal that gripped* Britain *in the* 1960s.

A Cardboard Congregation
Father Denham

Father Denham of Warleggan in Cornwall died in 1953, but for at least a decade before his demise no one had attended his regular Sunday services because of his incredibly rude manner. Unperturbed by this, Father Denham simply made life-sized parishioners out of cardboard and propped them up in the pews. Ramblers and visitors passing the church on Sundays could hear him delivering apparently passionate sermons to his cardboard flock.

So antisocial was Denham that he fitted a high barbed-wire fence around his house. It is difficult to say why he bothered because the vicarage did not contain a stick of furniture. The local villagers believed that Father Denham lived entirely on nettles and porridge.

Denham's problems probably stemmed from his bitterness and frustration at the Church's failure to promote him. He was posted to a remote part of Cornwall when he felt that he should have been elevated to a bishopric or given a living in a glamorous town. The fact that this didn't happen rankled, and over the years it became an obsession. Another problem was that Denham didn't like his real congregation – he thought that country folk were boorish, ill-educated and beneath him.

News of Denham's unusual conregation eventually reached Denham's bishop who was outraged that the parish priest was effectively being ignored by his flock. But the bishop knew that trying to get rid of the volatile Father Denham would almost certainly create an even bigger and noisier scandal, so he was left to his own devices. The Church authorities simply hoped that the cardboard congregation would keep Denham happy until the dear Lord chose to take him – and that's exactly what happened.

Licentious London –
Where not to be Seen

'I would be grateful to any of your readers who could tell me what I was doing between 1960 and 1974.'
Jeffrey Bernard

Sex and Debauchery South of the River
Southwark

Largely because it was outside the City of London's jurisdiction, Southwark gained a reputation from medieval times as a place of lawlessness and debauchery. However, from the point of view of ordinary Londoners it was a place of pleasure – which was why it was frowned upon by the respectable. When theatres were banned on the north bank of the Thames, they moved to Southwark. Shakespeare's Globe was first built at Shoreditch, but the landowner, a Puritan, refused to renew the players' lease so they quite literally dismantled the building and shipped it across the Thames where it was rebuilt in 1599.

But what really annoyed the Puritans and other fundamentalist Christians about Southwark was the huge number of brothels it contained. Of course, brothels existed because there was a huge demand for them, and there is no doubt that many an apparently respectable citizen who publicly condemned such institutions, also made regular use of them. In fact, that is the main reason they were never entirely suppressed.

BELOW: SOUTHWARK FAIR BY WILLIAM HOGARTH. LONDONERS CROSSED THE RIVER FOR SOUTHWARK'S THEATRES AND BROTHELS.

Brothels had originally existed in the City itself, but, like the theatres, they were expelled from the area. They found a natural home in what is now known as Bankside, alongside the bear pits and cock fights that made Elizabethan Southwark a byword for rough and illicit pleasures. Whenever modern developers dig beneath the soil in the area known as Bear Garden they come across large numbers of graves – these were the mass graves of the prostitutes who were not allowed burial in the churchyards.

Edward Alleyn (1566–1626), who founded Dulwich College in 1619, was famously keen on brothels and, indeed, he owned a number of them. A few of the smaller brothels – the Triple, the Bell, the Barge and the Cock – were owned by the theatre-owner Philip Henslowe (1550–1616). However, the real scandal of Southwark's brothels, or 'stews' as they were known, is that they were often owned by the Church! By far the biggest owner of such establishments was the Bishop of Winchester, who had a splendid palace in Southwark, the remains of which can still be seen today. The prostitutes in the area were known as the 'Bishop of Winchester's geese'.

The justification for this ownership – a justification that the Puritans of the mid-17th century refused to accept – was a quote from the theological philosopher Thomas Aquinas (c. 1225–74) who disliked prostitution but saw the necessity for it. Aquinas wrote that 'prostitution in the town is like the cesspool in a palace; take away the cesspool and the palace will become unclean and evil smelling'.

The general attitude to brothels was that they were essential. This is evident in the complete lack of embarrassment with which London's medieval map-makers recorded the name of one street famous for such establishments – it was known as Gropecunt Lane.

The Most Lawless Place in London
St Giles and Seven Dials

In the 18th century, Seven Dials, in the parish of St Giles-in-the-Fields, was a place of filth and squalor and debauchery and drunkenness. Tucked away between Covent Garden to the south and Bloomsbury to the north it miraculously escaped the wholesale redevelopment of the 1960s, and bears only a few scars from that unenlightened architectural period.

A medieval leper hospital once existed here, situated amid open fields and well away from the City of London. The developers arrived in the 17th century. They put up houses for artisans and skilled tradesmen, but within a few decades an area that had seemed a model development to Samuel Pepys, had degenerated into a dark, overcrowded and fearsome place.

ABOVE: *SEVEN DIALS WAS A NO-GO AREA EVEN FOR THE POLICE.*

Resurrection Gate

The old road to Oxford (now Oxford Street) runs along the northern extremity of the district; it passes close by the parish church of St Giles, who was patron saint of lepers. Nearby was Resurrection Gate, where for centuries the condemned took a last drink as they passed by on the journey from Newgate Prison in the east to the gallows at Tyburn (now Marble Arch) in the west. The Resurrection Gate – rebuilt in the 19th century and re-named the Angel Inn – is still next to St Giles' Church and you can follow the route of the old Oxford Road as it winds its way through what were once fields.

St Giles' Church was completed in 1712 after the earlier building began to collapse. The walls of the old church, which was built in the 12th century, had been undermined by the huge number of burials that had taken place there. The plague of 1665, probably the worst outbreak in the history of that terrible disease, began in St Giles.

By the 18th century, when William Hogarth depicted the area in his famous engraving 'Gin Lane', St Giles was a place avoided by anyone with the least pretensions to respectability. It was also pretty much beyond the reach of the authorities. Gin shops were everywhere and poverty and desperation made the inhabitants widely feared. If a criminal from the area was being taken from Newgate to Tyburn, extra soldiers were often drafted in to guard him because, as likely as not, his friends would mount a rescue operation as he stopped for his last drink at the Resurrection Gate. If he'd been carried off into the rookeries, as Seven Dials was then known, he would never be found.

The name Seven Dials comes from the place in the southern part of the district, where seven small streets meet to form a star. It was planned by Sir Thomas Neale and dates back to 1694. There is still a small market here every weekday – the market has been here for more than a century – and many of the houses in the surrounding streets date from the 18th century, although much altered.

The obelisk at the centre of the star where the streets meet is a modern replacement, but from here the narrow 18th-century streets radiate towards Covent Garden, Charing Cross Road, Shaftesbury Avenue and Long Acre. Many of the original rookeries were destroyed in the 1880s to make way for Shaftesbury Avenue and New Oxford Street, but a certain atmosphere of this once depraved part of London still lingers in the alleys and courtyards that survive.

Women and Children of the Night
Haymarket and Piccadilly

On a visit to London, the Great Russian novelist Fyodor Dostoevsky (1821–81) was horrified one night when a middle-aged woman in rags approached him in the Haymarket with a child aged no more than ten or eleven in tow. The woman told the author that he could have sex with the child in return for payment. Dostoevsky never forgot the incident and he realized immediately afterwards that the whole of the area around Haymarket and Piccadilly Circus was swarming with the poor and their children late at night because they were there to sell themselves.

Piccadilly is still famous for prostitution, but in the Victorian era it was particularly famous for child prostitution. Thousands of destitute families from London's tenements and slums had reached the stage where they had only one financial resource left – to sell their bodies. One writer noted that older women who were no longer attractive 'would offer to do the most unspeakable acts' in return for payment.

ABOVE: A Harlot's Progress *by* William Hogarth. *Prostitution was one of London's major industries.*

A City Industry

In his monumental work *London Labour and the London Poor* (1851), Henry Mayhew (1812–87) noted that prostitution was one of the capital's major industries, as with no social security or unemployment benefit a family could find themselves destitute overnight if the breadwinner lost his or her job or became too ill to work.

Victorian England was one of the wealthiest countries in the world, and it is scandalous that the authorities did not do more to protect its citizens from the inevitable ups and downs of the economy. The rich, while publicly condemning prostitution, were very often the people who patronized the prostitutes of Haymarket and elsewhere most eagerly.

One wealthy aristocrat of the time, known only as Walter, left a valuable collection of books to the British Library on the condition that it would also accept his multi-volume diary. This diary graphically detailed his contacts with thousands of prostitutes of all ages, including some from apparently respectable families who had fallen on hard times. What Walter most enjoyed was the fact that his money gave him absolute power over so many women. But there is one thing to be said in his favour – unlike so many wealthy men at the time he did not use the services of prostitutes and then condemn their way of life. He thought that in many ways they were better off than their sisters who were condemned to work 16-hour days in match factories or sewing for a tenth of what they could earn in one night in the Haymarket. 'I've spent some of my happiest hours with these so-called women of the streets,' he said 'and often found them intelligent and lively.'

> *'I've spent some of my happiest hours with these so-called women of the streets'*
> 'Walter'

Sex for Sale
Hyde Park

For middle- and upper-class men in 19th-century London, different districts offered different delights. 'Clubland', the architecturally grand area from Trafalgar Square to St James, was the place to meet like-minded people for lunch and dinner. It was also the place to make political connections or to receive and impart tips for insider dealing on the stock exchange.

At night, these areas were very different. If these well-off gentlemen wanted to have sex with children they set off for Haymarket (see above), where youngsters of both sexes were readily available. If they preferred a more mature woman they might visit Soho or Shepherd Market. But if they wanted oral sex the only place to go was Hyde Park.

Hyde Park, which still extends to more than 350 acres, was originally owned by the monks of Westminster Abbey, but the land was confiscated by Henry VIII (1509–47) when the monastery was suppressed in 1536. Henry used the park exclusively as a hunting ground. In the centuries following his death it continued to be used for hunting, the only difference being that the quarry had changed. Where Henry had pursued deer, the 19th-century rake pursued women. One commentator of the time put the number of people fornicating in Hyde Park on an average summer evening well into the hundreds.

By the 1890s, Hyde Park's reputation for prostitution reached its zenith, but the nature of the prostitutes operating in the park had changed. Under cover of darkness older women offered oral sex to almost anyone passing by. One 'respectable' night wanderer recalled being propositioned more than a dozen times during a walk that lasted 'no more than twenty minutes'.

In the corner of Hyde Park nearest to Marble Arch, an entirely different kind of sexual thrill was offered – that of cottaging. The public lavatories here were famous throughout the gay world for decades and, until the police intervened in the 1980s, queues formed in the evenings as patrons came from far and wide to enjoy illicit sex with complete strangers.

Drunken Duels

In the 18th and 19th centuries, Hyde Park had other scandals to offer, too. It was the scene of numerous illegal duels. Drunken officers from nearby barracks in Knightsbridge would insult each other and then fight with either swords or pistols. Despite being illegal, duelling continued until the end of the 19th century – if one of the duellers was badly injured or even killed he was taken away by his friends and a story invented to account for his injuries.

10 Rillington Place
John Christie

The murders that occurred at 10 Rillington Place in Notting Hill more than 50 years ago shocked the nation and led to the execution of an innocent man, Timothy Evans. Evans's execution was undoubtedly instrumental in bringing capital punishment to an end in Britain.

The real killer was a Yorkshireman named John Christie. After being badly injured during the First World War, he became a postman in his native Halifax. He married in 1920, but began to get into trouble and was prosecuted in 1923 for obtaining money by false pretences. By the mid-1920s Christie was living in London without his wife. After another prison sentence for attacking a prostitute with whom he lived, Christie persuaded his wife to join him in London and the couple moved to Rillington Place in 1938.

In 1943, while his wife was away visiting relatives, Christie appears to have had sex with a prostitute and then strangled her. He buried her under the floorboards. No motive for the murder was ever discovered. A year later, Christie persuaded a colleague at the electrical factory at which he worked to visit him. While pretending to treat her asthma, he gassed her before having sex with her, strangling her and burying her in the garden.

WHAT HAPPENED TO THE WOMEN AT 10 RILLINGTON PLACE?

Mass Murder

In 1948, Timothy Evans moved into a flat in the same house with his wife, Beryl and their infant daughter. Christie befriended them, but in 1949 Beryl and her daughter were murdered. All the evidence now suggests that Christie killed them, but Evans was tried for the crime and hanged. It was easy for Christie to implicate the young man, who had the intelligence of an 11-year-old and could barely write his own name.

In 1952, Christie murdered his wife and a year later he murdered a prostitute, wedging her body into a small gap between an outside lavatory and the wall. By now he had few other places to secrete his victims – his wife was under the floorboards and there were bodies in the garden and behind the shed.

After two more murders Christie's luck ran out. With nowhere left to hide bodies, he left the house in Rillington Place. The badly concealed remains of his victims were discovered by a tenant a few days later. Christie was arrested wandering aimlessly around London, tried and hanged. In 1966, Evans was given a posthumous pardon, a year after the death penalty was abolished in Britain for all crimes other than treason. No. 10 Rillington Place was eventually demolished, although for years after the murders it was an essential stop on any tour of west London's more gruesome sights.

Bohemian Soho
Julian Maclaren Ross & Co.

While the rest of Britain slumbered on in the post-war period, largely concerned with keeping up with the Joneses, maintaining a clean front doorstep and high-quality net curtains, Soho's inhabitants lived the lives that they had always lived – lives of excess, drinking, promiscuity and drug taking.

Numerous writers have described Soho in the late 1940s and 1950s. The gay experience has been documented by Quentin Crisp (see pages 79–80) and the painter Daniel Farson, while Julian Maclaren Ross (1912–64) gives perhaps the best picture of heterosexual life in what was then Britain's most scandalous locale.

Ross was a minor author who published a number of stories and forgotten novels, but his *Memoir of the Forties* is a classic of Soho literature. It describes the people and locations, the pubs, prostitutes and illegal drinking dens that characterized an area that suburban clergymen regularly warned their parishioners to avoid at all costs if, as one vicar put it, 'they valued their souls and the life to come'.

Ross describes the steps into the Horseshoe Club where he and Dylan Thomas (see pages 81–4) used to drink and down which numerous drunken writers fell. He describes an inebriated Caitlin Thomas wrestling with the poet Louis MacNeice to avoid going to Broadcasting House. He also recalls the eccentric poetry editor J. Meary Tambimuttu, or Tambi as he was known, who trawled Soho's bars and clubs offering advances to anyone who'd claimed they'd written a book while a crowd of acolytes trailed continually behind him.

Tambimutti's office, which was in the basement of a slimy Soho tenement, consisted of a few broken items of furniture and piles of unsolicited manuscripts, which he explained were gradually being gnawed at by rats so there was no real point in sending them back. Tambi was certainly one of Soho's most outrageous characters at the time. He never asked to borrow money, instead suggesting in a commanding voice that companions should hand over any cash that they happened to have. Most complied without a word.

Pub Crawling

Tambi and fellow habitués of the area would stagger from pub to pub between Soho proper and that equally disreputable northern extension of the area, Fitzrovia, just to the north of Oxford Street. According to Ross, wherever one went in the 1940s, faded beauties and artists' models were drunk and asleep in pub corners or gutters; writers were shouting, arguing or falling over; and painters, such as Robert Colquhoun and Robert MacBryde, were fighting, either with each other or with anyone else who came to hand. Nina Hamnet (1890–1956), a talented painter and former artist's model, gradually drank herself to death in Soho.

The last of the great Soho characters, the journalist Jeffrey Bernard (1932–97), slowly drank himself to death in the Coach and Horses on the corner of Greek Street and Romilly Street. But compared to some of his contemporaries, he had staying power – by the time he finally fell off his bar stool for the last time in the late 1990s, he had long been the last of the post-war generation that had found Soho so congenial.

The Slum Landlord
Peter Rachman

Changes in the law to protect tenants from unscrupulous landlords were pushed through parliament largely as a result of the activities of one man: Peter Rachman (1920–63). His business practices were so notorious that 'Rachmanism' has its own entry in the Oxford English Dictionary, where it is defined as 'buying up slums to fill with immigrants at extortionate rents'.

Rachman was born into a Jewish family in Poland. He escaped to England when the Nazi terror began, although he'd already spent some months in a Russian camp where he was treated appallingly. Given his own background as an immigrant it is extraordinary that Rachman later treated the tenants in his own houses so badly.

Rachman's name became synonymous with appalling housing in 1950s Notting Hill, which was a poor, run-down area at the time. He bought his first house near Ladbroke Grove and immediately packed West Indian immigrants into it. Soon he was buying up other properties, until his empire encompassed some 100 houses, most of which were in the Notting Hill Gate area. He took full advantage of the mass arrival of vulnerable immigrants, which coincided with a relaxation of the tenancy laws by the Conservative government in 1957. Basically this allowed a landlord to increase rents as much as he or she liked. If Rachman's tenants caused him the least problem or refused to do exactly as he wished he would go to any lengths to remove them – one tenant awoke to find that the roof of his house had been removed by Rachman's cronies during the night.

Rachman's brutality was notorious. If tenants so much as demurred at a hefty rent increase or refused to leave one of his properties he sent his goons round to intimidate them. Only one other landlord, Nicholas Van Hoogstraten (born 1946) – who famously described his tenants as 'scum' – has been able to give the landlord–tenant relationship such a bad reputation.

Rachman, Ronnie and Reggie

Rachman was never prosecuted for ill-treating his tenants – largely because he covered his tracks so well. However, he met his match in the Kray twins who decided that Rachman should be paying them protection money. Rachman refused to pay, only to find his burly enforcers beaten up by some even nastier characters employed by the Krays. Rachman responded by giving the Krays a gambling club.

Rachman also became involved with some of the most scandalous call girls of the era – Christine Keeler and Mandy Rice-Davies (see pages 158–9) were both his mistresses. He was also convicted of earning money from brothels, but despite the best efforts of the police, little evidence of his strong-arm tactics against his tenants could be found.

In the 1960s, some respite came for his hard-pressed tenants when Rachman sold all his Notting Hill Gate properties. In 1963, he did the only decent thing he appears to have done in his life: he died. However, there was speculation that he hadn't died at all but had disappeared to avoid prosecution. Thankfully, Rachman has never reappeared.

Drug Taking and Free Love
Portobello Road

The sexual revolution of the 1960s was an enormous shock to the values and attitudes of the parents of those whose culture came to be typified by the hippie movement. It was a movement that threw out almost everything the older generation had valued and admired. Clothing changed beyond all recognition, drug-taking became common, work was no longer seen as important unless it was something you really wanted to do, and the insistence that sex, love, marriage and children were a package vanished overnight.

In 1960s London, the centre of this new world of free love was undoubtedly the area around Notting Hill Gate and Portobello Road in west London, where new bands played electronic music that baffled older residents. Groups of youngsters hung out smoking dope and made love on principle to anyone they happened to meet – or at least that was how the area's hippie scene was perceived.

The movement was also influenced by the philosophies of the East, an influence most famously advocated by the Beatles, each member of which seemed to have his own Indian guru at one stage. Indian clothing – masses of which was available in shops up and down Portobello Road – came to influence the hippie style of dress.

The length of male hair was one of the most scandalous aspects of the new movement – it got longer and longer, and blurred the distinction between the sexes, much to the horror of churchmen, teachers and other 'pillars of the community'. Older parliamentarians condemned the new attitudes to sex and drugs, but, of course, nothing could be done. The old deference to authority had gone – and drugs, promiscuity and Portobello Road were to blame, so far as they could see.

The Sexual Revolution

The sexual revolution, which was so central to the idea of free love, actually had its origins in the late 1940s and 1950s, when academic reports into human sexuality shocked people on both sides of the Atlantic. The 1948 Kinsey Report showed that about ten per cent of the population was probably gay and that masturbation was almost universal. The Establishment was horrified, and the situation only got worse when Masters and Johnson published a survey in the late 1950s that made the whole subject of orgasms – particularly the female variety – a topic that could be discussed openly. Prior to that it was officially considered rather disgusting that a respectable woman should actually enjoy having sex.

Of course, sexual inhibitions were loosened considerably by the huge availability of marijuana and psychedelic drugs such as LSD, as well as with the advent of the contraceptive pill. The whole hippie philosophy was a hedonist's dream and the only rule was 'If it feels good do it'.

As men's hair got longer, women's skirts got shorter. The arrival of the mini-skirt in the mid-1960s caused further anguish to the older generation. But the old world was dead and drug taking became and has remained a part of youth culture. Portobello Road has changed now, but it was once at the heart of one of the most thoroughgoing sexual revolutions in history.

The Political World –
Westminster's Seedy Side

'My life has been one
long descent into
respectability'
Mandy Rice-Davies

The Philandering Civil Servant
Samuel Pepys

The diaries of Samuel Pepys (1633–1703) lay unpublished from the time of his death until the early 19th century, when the great man's bizarre shorthand and crabbed script were deciphered. When Pepys's notebooks were finally published, they were carefully edited to screen the public from the scandalous revelations they contained – revelations that only came to light much later when the unexpurgated text was finally published in the 20th century.

A Bit Of What He Fancied

Pepys had a successful career as a civil servant, rising to Secretary of the Admiralty during the reign of Charles II. But he was also a serial philanderer who, as his diaries revealed, attempted to have sex with anyone he fancied. His journal is full of entries that describe him fondling his servants' breasts or trying to get them to hold his penis. The curious thing is that in each of these amorous adventures, Pepys seems to have felt that it was completely unnecessary to engage in any conversation before lunging at his victim. There is no doubt that he got away with his outrageous behaviour because he either molested his own female servants – who knew that he would sack them if they complained – or his social inferiors who were likely to be overawed by his expensive clothes and gentleman-like bearing.

However, on at least one occasion a victim got the better of him. Pepys describes brazenly walking up to a woman in church and beginning to fondle her. She moved away without saying a word and when he attempted to follow her she pulled out a pin and threatened him with it!

When travelling by coach, Pepys would grasp the hand of any female passenger present – even if he'd never met or spoken to her before – and try to

RIGHT: *Samuel Pepys's diaries were x-rated until recently.*

place it on his penis. On one journey he got away with such behaviour while his wife sat beside him!

All of this was meticulously recorded in his diary. His sexual revelations were written in a curious mix of Spanish and French. For example, after taking a pregnant friend of his wife home in a coach he confessed that he 'did tocar mi cosa con su mano through my chemise, but yet so as to hazer me hazer la grande cosa'. Translated, this means that he made her place her hand inside his breeches, but not so successfully that he was able to have an orgasm. The diaries are packed with incidents like these – some of which involve young girls who in today's society would be under-age.

In another episode, Pepys described a shameful business in which a shipbuilder at the Navy yard offered him sex with his wife in return for extra work and more pay! The poor woman loved her husband and did not want to take part in the scheme, but she had no choice and Pepys received extra satisfaction from the fact that he could do as he pleased with her whether she liked it or not.

Although we relish their bawdy immediacy now, the early 19th-century academics who first translated the diaries were horrified. The idea that a sober and very senior civil servant could carry on like this and write every detail down was disgusting to the translators. Again and again in the original transcript the word 'obj' appears – meaning that pornographic or objectionable passages have been omitted. In fact, as late as the 1950s, editions of the diaries included the line 'suitably edited' on the frontispiece – just in case anyone should doubt the nature of the contents.

The Rights of Man
Thomas Paine

In 1791, Thomas Paine (1737–1809) published the first part of his radical book, *The Rights of Man*. It would arouse little comment today, as so much of what he advocated has come to pass – universal male suffrage, pensions and maternity rights, for example, are now accepted without question. But when the pamphlet was published, Paine became the most notorious man in Britain and he was forced to leave the country or risk arrest and possible execution. Paine's crime was to question the status quo – the inherent belief that the rich and aristocratic deserved their wealth simply because they were born to it.

Thomas Paine was born the son of a Quaker corset maker in Thetford, Norfolk. A precocious child, he was sent to the local grammar school before becoming an apprentice to his father and later a teacher. However, it was while working as a government customs and excise official that his sense of outrage at the injustice of the prevailing system first came to the fore. In 1774, Paine demanded an increase in salary for himself and his colleagues and was promptly sacked. Disgusted, he moved to London and published a pamphlet criticizing his old employers. It was at about this time that Paine met the American statesman Benjamin Franklin (1706–90), who was living in London. Franklin persuaded Paine that he should travel to America.

In America, he wrote numerous articles that expounded theories that were then seen as radical or even revolutionary. He advocated an end to slavery, criticized the British monarchy and argued for the independence of the American colonies. By 1781, he had travelled to France to raise support for American independence. Back in America he continued to earn his living as a journalist before returning to Britain in 1787.

The Voice of Reason

The publication of *The Rights of Man*, a 'scandalous, seditious book', caused outrage. Among the most shocking parts of the book was an obvious attack on the high born, in which Paine stated that 'taxes on the very necessaries of life enable an endless tribe of idle princes and princesses to pass with stupid pomp before a gaping crowd.'

Today, Paine's ideas seem perfectly reasonable, but his criticism of hereditary government was deemed seditious libel at the time. In truth, the government was afraid that if they did not suppress the book it might encourage an uprising similar to the French Revolution. *The Rights of Man* was banned, but Paine managed to escape to France before the net closed round him. Ironically, the government's reaction made the book far more popular than it might otherwise have been. Its popularity was also helped by the fact that Paine gave up all rights in the work and announced that anyone who wanted to could print it free of charge.

Despite being hailed as a hero in France, Paine found himself in prison there in 1793, as he had criticized the execution of Louis XVI. It was only the intervention of the Americans that saved him from the guillotine.

Ever his own man, Paine continued to write whatever struck him as true, and in 1795 he published *The Age of Reason*, his most revolutionary work to date. The work argued against the perceived truth of Christianity and stated that the Old Testament was immoral and that much of the Bible was contradictory.

By now, Paine had upset people on both sides of the Atlantic and the English Channel. Despite his support for the colonies during their war for independence, his attacks on Christianity alienated the more devout Americans. Paine faded into virtual obscurity. He died in 1809, by which time more than 1.5 million copies of *The Rights of Man* had been sold.

The Mistress in the Closet
Charles Stewart Parnell

The huge problems of England's relationship with Ireland might have been solved but for a scandal more than a century ago that rocked the Palace of Westminster and swept one of the Emerald Isle's most charismatic leaders from power. Charles Stewart Parnell (1846–91) was an enormously powerful orator who, by 1886, had persuaded parliament to at least consider the idea of Irish Home Rule. This was no mean feat given the absolute opposition to the idea by many members of the House of Lords, some of whom enjoyed considerable rents from their Irish estates.

Parnell was born in Wicklow. After studying at a private school in Yeovil, Somerset, he went on to Cambridge University, but left without taking his degree. In 1874, he joined the Home Government Party and a year later was elected a Member of Parliament. In 1879, Parnell helped to found the Irish National Land League with Michael Davitt (1846–1906). The league had a number of successes against English landlords, some of whom demanded extortionate rents from their tenants and could evict them at a moment's notice. Parnell was arrested for incitement and imprisoned under the terms of the Coercion Act in 1881, but he was released after signing a private deal with the Prime Minister, William Gladstone (1809–98) the following year.

In 1886, the first Home Rule bill was defeated in Parliament. However, the mere fact that it had been put before Parliament showed that the cause of Irish republicanism had come a long way.

There is no doubt that both the House of Commons and the House of Lords were becoming seriously worried by Parnell's growing fame and popularity in Ireland, so they must have been delighted when the clouds of controversy began to gather around the great Irish leader in 1888.

Parnell's Downfall

A series of compromising letters about Parnell had been published by *The Times*. The letters had been forged, but the investigation into their publication concluded with a shocking piece of information – Parnell had been cited as correspondent in a divorce case. His mistress of nine years and mother of his children, Kitty O' Shea, was being sued for divorce by her husband, William. Despite the fact that the divorce was a private matter and that Parnell later married Kitty, Parnell's political career was in ruins.

Parnell's case wasn't helped by the fact that another series of forged letters he is purported to have written to his mistress supported the assassination of the Chief Secretary of Ireland. Married to his beloved Kitty for little more than a year, Parnell died in 1891.

The scandal is said to have put the cause of Irish Home Rule back at least a generation – as the consequences of the affair reverberated for years. The Irish Parliamentary Party was split and Liberal MPs who had supported Home Rule dropped their support for it. Even Parnell's own party thought that their leader's private life was more important than the cause to which they'd devoted their lives. Victorian morality had triumphed.

Lloyd George's Gorgeous Girls
David Lloyd George

Despite his strict Nonconformist upbringing, David Lloyd George (1863–1945), one of the greatest Prime Ministers of the 20th century, led a double life. While the woman to whom he was legally married lived in the family house in Criccieth, Wales, Lloyd George lived openly with his mistress, Frances Stevenson, and their daughter in another residence on the outskirts of London.

Lloyd George pushed through some of the most radical parliamentary reforms in history – including the first bill to give the elderly pensions and social security – all in the face of entrenched opposition in the House of Lords. He was frequently accused of double-dealing. Having apparently supported pacifism before the First World War, he backed the use of force when hostilities broke out, leading a coalition government throughout the conflict. He also supported the Irish nationalist cause, although he refused to support the idea of independence for Wales. He spoke up for the poor, but hated the idea of being without money – with two families to maintain this is hardly surprising.

Lloyd George was also accused of selling political honours (see page 163). He handed out more gongs to his friends than any other Prime Minister until Tony Blair.

Were a modern Prime Minister to live with his mistress, he would almost certainly be ousted from power, but after the First World War a curious atmosphere of deference clouded the media's view of prominent men, and their private lives were rarely mentioned. Having been elected a Member of Parliament at the tender age of 27, Lloyd George escaped public criticism for his unconventional private life and was eventually made Father of the House of Commons.

> *'There are greater storms in politics than you will ever find at sea.'*
>
> *David Lloyd George*

ABOVE: *David Lloyd George lived a double life with his mistress.*

The Monocled Dandy
Maundy Gregory

Arthur Maundy Gregory (1877–1941) was at the centre of one of the worst political scandals of the 20th century – he may also, quite literally, have got away with murder. Born to a clergyman father, Gregory studied at Oxford, leaving early to join MI5 in 1909. He later worked for MI6 where, although he was hired to keep an eye on suspicious foreigners, he actually discovered far more about British politicians and other members of the Establishment. Much of what he discovered involved sexual misdemeanours, and he was later accused of having blackmailed various people, although nothing was ever proved against him.

In 1918, Gregory was asked by the head of Special Branch to keep an eye on Victor Grayson, a former MP who was suspected of having IRA sympathies and working for the Bolsheviks in Russia. The tables were quickly turned, as Grayson discovered he was being observed. Grayson began to spy on his watcher – and what he discovered horrified him.

At a public meeting, Grayson accused the Prime Minister, David Lloyd George (see page 150), of selling political honours via an intermediary whom he didn't name, but described as a 'monocled dandy with offices in Whitehall'. He also indicated that when the time was right he would name the man. Why he didn't name Gregory there and then is a mystery, but in the ensuing scandal, Gregory must have known he was in constant danger of exposure. In September 1920, Grayson was attacked and badly beaten. His assailants were never caught, but Grayson refused to give up his campaign against Lloyd George and the corruption of the honours system.

A Mysterious End

While drinking with friends at the end of September that same year, Grayson received a mysterious phone call and left for a meeting in Leicester Square. He was seen entering a house by the Thames that was later identified as the home of Maundy Gregory. Grayson was never seen again and his body was not found.

The monocled dandy continued to sell political honours, but in 1932 he overstepped the mark and offered a knighthood – at a price – to a Commander Leake. Having shown enough interest to gather sufficient evidence, Leake went to the police. On being arrested, Gregory immediately contacted the rich and famous who had bought honours from him in the past and threatened to expose them unless they paid for his silence. They must have paid well because Gregory gave no evidence and was sent down for two years.

Perhaps the most disgraceful aspect of the whole affair was that when he left prison Gregory was spirited away to France and the British Conservative Party awarded him a pension of £2,000 a year for the rest of his life.

The British Fascist
Oswald Mosley

Diana Mosley (1910–2004) was one of the celebrated Mitford sisters (see pages 210–12) and, with the dogged determination that so characterized her family, she defended her husband's reputation to the end of her long life. Oswald Ernald Mosley (1896–1980) was a superb orator with enormous charisma. His political judgement was non-existent, but his speeches were said to arouse an almost religious fervour in those listening, whether they were convinced or unconvinced by his beliefs. Political grandees from all parties pronounced him one of the greatest men of his age, and many in the Labour party confidently predicted that he would be their future leader.

There is no doubt that Mosley was a curious mix. He combined some odd beliefs – he believed in both socialism and the Empire, in high wages and short hours for the working classes and in social justice rather than profit. He felt he could solve the huge problem of unemployment, which had hitherto been ignored by parliament. Indeed, Mosley attacked the Conservative leader Stanley Baldwin (1867–1947) when he said that the working classes would have to take a cut in wages but said nothing about the rich cutting their profits.

Thoroughly disenchanted with Labour politics, Mosley founded the British Union of Fascists in 1932. He viewed fascism as the way to unite all classes in a movement for equality and justice. It was considered an extremely provocative move and he was condemned on all sides. It is certainly true that the Nazi-style salute and banners did not help his cause, although it is worth

BELOW: *OSWALD MOSLEY WAS IMPRISONED DURING WORLD WAR TWO FOR HIS POLITICAL BELIEFS AND SUPPORT OF HITLER.*

remembering that fascism did not quite have the reputation then that it has today, and Hitler certainly had his admirers in Britain at the time. Mosley's fascism was based on the idea that one strong man could lead the people out of the wilderness and unite the Empire.

Soon after the Second World War broke out in 1939, Mosley and Diana were imprisoned, solely, he claimed, for opposing the war. In fact, their support for Hitler was the real reason. With the war over, Mosley continued to speak and write on politics, but he was shunned as yesterday's man. In 1966, he was still writing about the need for a government that united all sides, but no one was listening.

Cold War Cadets
Burgess, Philby, Maclean and Blunt

The biggest political scandal of the 20th century was undoubtedly the discovery that a group of Establishment figures had spent years passing British secrets to the Russians. More has probably been written about Guy Burgess (1911–63), Kim Philby (1912–88), Anthony Blunt (1907–83) and Donald Maclean (1913–83) than about any other comparable group of Englishmen. Their motives have been picked over again and again by writers as diverse as Chapman Pincher and Graham Greene.

What made the scandal particularly extraordinary was that many years passed between the authorities discovering that these men were possibly involved in espionage and anyone actually doing anything about it. For example, Philby was sacked from the secret service for his probable involvement in the defection of Burgess and Maclean in 1951 – and then promptly reinstated! The difficulty for MI5 and MI6 was that the spies weren't perceived as the sort of individuals who would normally have come under suspicion for having Communist sympathies – they were Cambridge graduates with impeccable backgrounds. Even when they did come under suspicion many thought there must be a mistake. As a result, a vast amount of damage was done to the British security services, whose reputation was severely damaged and even now the American secret services still don't quite trust either MI5 or MI6.

Cambridge Spies

Burgess, Philby, Maclean and Blunt met at Trinity College Cambridge in the 1930s. Today, it is difficult to understand the political ferment of that decade, but memoirs of the time remind us that Communism was still considered by many to be a logical and reasonable answer to world poverty, injustice and

AMERICAN FEARS ON BRITISH SECURITY

Burgess and Maclean Case Likely to Harden Attitude to Atomic Secrets

25 SEP 1955

SUN-TIMES By NICHOLAS CARROLL,
The Sunday Times Diplomatic Correspondent

THE Government belated admissions in the case of Burgess and

---

ister
y tale

19 SEP. 55

or later almost

DAILY EXPRE
The Daily Express
guardian of p
liberties, and it
duty to perfor
enlightening the p

24 SEP. 55

OPINIO

WHO ARE
GUILTY M

IT is an in
dorum t

---

the Chronicle

LURE ALL
HE WAY

per on Burgess and Maclean is an

THE FOREIGN OFFICE SCANDAL

Buckets and buckets and buckets of whitewash

24 SEP. 55

WHODUNIT?

Don't ask the chaps at the Foreign Office—THEY DON'T KNOW!

DAILY HER

Wrong
20 SEP 1955
right ti

LL the Foreign Office ne
to find microfilm of its se

THE TIMES

ATE AND TOO
LITTLE
24 SEP 55

s call for comment," says
per on MACLEAN and
t is typical of its prim-
siveness There are not
en points that call for

Comment

MONDAY, NOVEMBER 7, 1955

LESS DOPE, PLEASE

OUR advice to Govern-
ment and Foreign
Office in the Maclean and
debate way is :

---

25 OCT 1955

News the Chronicle

THE NATION MUS
BE TOLD

MENT reassembles today in the se

---

ily
rror

FORWARD
WITH THE PEOPLE

Today Parliament will discuss

THE FOREIGN FICE SCANDAL

TODAY Parliament has a straight question

MIRROR

6 Daily Telegraph and

THE DAILY TELEGRAPH

MORNING POST

DAILY TELEGRAPH - June 29
MORNING POST - November 2
AMALGAMATED October 1 19

TUESDAY, NOVEMBER 8, 19
135 Fleet Street, London EC
Telephone: Fleet Street 4242

A SQUALID CASE AND ITS LESSONS

WHY has the Burgess-Maclean
case continued to excite pu
Not because

unemployment. It was also seen by many as the only alternative to fascism, which was rising throughout Europe. The true nature of Stalin's Russia had not yet come to light, which is why the four were – at least as students – unashamedly left-leaning in their sympathies.

The Russian secret service, the NKVD, saw these outspoken young Cambridge students as a gift. Blunt was recruited first and went on to recruit others on behalf of the NKVD. Fluent in French, Blunt became one of Britain's most brilliant art historians, eventually accepting the role of surveyor of the Queen's pictures and a knighthood, although he never abandoned his early political sympathies. In the early 1960s, he agreed to confess in return for immunity from prosecution.

Blunt managed to hide his espionage activities from the public until 1979, when Mrs Thatcher named him in Parliament and he was stripped of his knighthood. Blunt never apologized for his actions, and a glance at the transcripts of his interrogation following his confession reveals that he was evasive and only named spies who were either dead or beyond the reach of the authorities. His commitment to the cause was baffling because he would undoubtedly have loathed actually living in Communist Russia.

Guy Burgess, a foreign office secretary in Washington and London, was the least stable of the Cambridge spies. He was a promiscuous homosexual and an extremely unpredictable alcoholic. Nevertheless, Burgess had a large number of devoted friends and admirers who gave him access to secrets and protected him. After he defected to Russia in 1951, he spent ten miserable years living in a country he found utterly uncongenial – a situation that was brilliantly portrayed in Alan Bennett's play based on Burgess' life, *An Englishman Abroad*.

Donald Maclean, a foreign office secretary in Paris, was brilliant, but like Burgess he was also an alcoholic. He was far less emotionally stable than the other men, and it was Kim Philby's belief that Maclean would crack quickly under interrogation that led to Maclean's defection in 1951.

The Third Man

Philby, who worked as a journalist and an MI6 agent, and achieved immortality as Graham Greene's 'Third Man' in both print and film, has been described as the greatest spy ever. Certainly he was something of a chameleon and could play any part to perfection. He claimed to have recruited Maclean and Philby, although there is no evidence to back this up. He married four times and after his defection in 1963 lived happily in Moscow until his death. He spent his time in Russia training other spies and his portrait even appeared on a Russian stamp. He was an active spy from 1940 to 1963 and his espionage certainly led to the deaths of many British and American agents.

RIGHT: KIM PHILBY, ONE OF THE NOTORIOUS 'CAMBRIDGE SPIES'.

The worst of the damage Philby and his associates committed was done during the Second World War, when all three were passing details of Allied military strategy to Moscow. Philby also told the Russians that the British had broken the Enigma code.

The American discovery of the existence of a British agent known only as Homer led to the defection of Burgess and Maclean. If Maclean confessed, Philby knew the game would be up for the entire cell, so he arranged for Burgess to be sent back to London from his post in Washington where he was told to defect. Burgess was ordered to remain, but he ignored this order and Philby never forgave him. In May 1951, Burgess and Maclean vanished, reappearing in Moscow. The British government was so embarrassed they could barely bring themselves to admit that the two had done anything wrong at all.

As Burgess had been living with Philby in Washington, Philby came under suspicion but he remained silent under interrogation. He was forced to resign from MI6, although some time later he was re-employed. In 1955, the Prime Minister, Harold Macmillan, publicly cleared Philby of being 'the Third Man'. In 1963, confronted by an old friend who had fresh evidence, Philby confessed. Incredibly, he was given a few days to prepare for his return to England and used that time to defect to Russia. The final scandal of the whole sorry saga is that the British government may well have allowed him to flee, rather than undergo the embarrassment of a prosecution and trial.

The Profumo Affair
John Profumo

If there can be said to be such a thing then the Profumo Affair was the perfect scandal. It had everything – a beautiful woman, an aristocratic politician, a Russian secret service agent and a 'Mr Fixit' who appears to have arranged regular orgies for members of the Establishment.

At the heart of the scandal, which broke in 1963 at the height of the Cold War, was the affair between Oxford-educated Secretary of State for War, John Profumo (born 1915) and Christine Keeler (born 1942), a former showgirl. The problem was not just the affair – although Profumo was married – it was the fact that Keeler was also sleeping with the Russian defence attaché Eugene Ivanov. Even if state secrets were not at risk during the lovers' pillowtalk, security had been compromised. Profumo had to go.

There had been a time when an eminent politician caught in such a scandal would have been able to have a word with a few old school friends in Fleet Street and kept the story under wraps. But by 1963, Fleet Street was manned by a new breed of editor that had no real connection with the Establishment. The tenor of the times had changed and the culture of deference to the rich, powerful and aristocratic had been overtaken by a desire to dish the dirt. And that's certainly what the papers did with Profumo and Keeler. They railed at the hypocrisy of the upper classes and dug up every bit of muck they could.

The Political Pimp

Behind the story of Profumo's downfall was an odder and even more sordid story. Keeler and a fellow showgirl, Mandy Rice-Davies, had been groomed by the Svengali-like Stephen Ward, who introduced the women to the rich and famous. Ward also organized orgies, at which one cabinet minister – yet to be identified – allegedly ate from a dog bowl on the floor and served drinks while naked except for a mask.

Ward arranged liaisons for both women and he was eventually charged with living off immoral earnings – in other words, he was running a brothel. Keeler and Rice-Davies gave evidence at Ward's trial and stated that he did indeed arrange orgies, but in order to gain influence rather than make money. Ward was never found guilty, as he committed suicide before the jury could make up their minds. Keeler eventually served nine months in prison for an unrelated offence.

Other than Profumo, no one in high office suffered as a result of the scandal, although Harold Macmillan resigned as Prime Minister shortly afterwards. Profumo's real mistake was to lie to parliament – when first confronted he said he had only been on friendly terms with Christine Keeler,

ABOVE: *MANDY RICE-DAVIES, THE SHOWGIRL WHO SLEPT WITH THE ARISTOCRAT, LORD ASTOR.*

but a week or so later he was forced to admit to the affair. There was no real surprise when Lord Denning's report into the matter contained nothing more than a mild rebuke for the government for not dealing with it more speedily.

Christine Keeler and Mandy Rice-Davies were certainly used as the playthings of the rich but neither will ever be forgotten. Keeler is one of the icons of the 1960s and when Rice-Davies heard that Lord Astor had denied sleeping with her she uttered the immortal line: 'Well he would, wouldn't he?'.

The Lord and the Prime Minister's Wife
Lord Boothby

To read Robert, later Lord, Boothby's official biography is to be impressed at his long devotion to public service and his gradual climb up the greasy pole. While it is true that he was never going to be Prime Minister, he was knighted and took a seat in the House of Lords, which is pretty good going for a man whose private life was riddled with scandal.

Lord Boothby (1900–1986) once confessed to the gangster Ronnie Kray, who was a personal friend, that he could never make up his mind whether he liked young boys or young girls best. Certainly, the Krays and Boothby's other associates managed to procure a string of young men and women for the ageing peer's pleasure.

An Un-extraordinary Background

Boothby was born in Scotland. After an education at Eton and Oxford he joined the Conservative Party and was elected MP for East Aberdeenshire in 1924. He was Winston Churchill's private secretary for three years in the 1920s, and supported Churchill's insistence that far more money should be spent on defence. He met Hitler in 1932 and was immediately convinced that the German leader was mad. As he was leaving at the end of their meeting the Führer's arm shot into the air and he shouted 'Heil Hitler'. Boothby's response was to shoot his own arm into the air and shout 'Heil Boothby'!

He joined the Air Force during the Second World War, worked for the Council for United Europe from 1949–54 and was knighted in 1953. Like his friend Tom Driberg (1905–76), who also had a colourful private life, he enjoyed a long and successful political career and no real hint of his affairs ever reached the public. In addition to his association with the Krays – he once spoke up on their behalf in the House of Lords – he was an enthusiast for cottaging (meeting men in public lavatories for anonymous sex).

Boothby also had a long affair with Lady Dorothy Macmillan, the wife of Harold, who was Prime Minister between 1957 and 1963. Boothby certainly made her pregnant on at least one occasion and there has always been the strong suggestion that he was the father of one or more of her four

LEFT: LORD BOOTHBY MANAGED TO LIVE A SCANDALOUS LIFE WITHOUT EVER BEING EXPOSED.

children. Boothby was one of those rare politicians who through luck, charm and great care was never exposed as the philanderer he was.

The Maida Vale Prostitutes
Lord Lambton

If it hadn't been a tragedy for him personally, the story of Lord Lambton's downfall in 1973 would be rather amusing – in a classic sting he was photographed in bed with not one but two prostitutes. To add to the scandal, he was also smoking a joint.

Lord Lambton, son of the Earl of Durham and cousin to Foreign Secretary Sir Alec Douglas Home, had been MP for Berwick on Tweed since 1950. He and his wife, Belinda Blew Jones, lived in a Georgian mansion in Mayfair where she entertained the good and the great on a lavish scale. The small flat in Maida Vale in which he was photographed entertained a similar clientèle, as it was regularly filled with the rich and powerful – or at least that was what Lambton later told his superiors. The apartment in question was owned by Norma Russell, one of a group of about 15 prostitutes who serviced rich and aristocratic clients.

The sting began when Russell's husband, Colin Levy, realized who Lambton was and contacted the *News of the World*. The paper sent a photographer to the flat who secretly snapped the MP. However, the newspaper eventually decided not to print the pictures, so Levy didn't receive the payoff for which he'd hoped even though the story itself was doing the rounds on Fleet Street and was soon public knowledge.

Escaping Boredom

After his fall from grace, Lambton maintained that the only reason he'd consorted with prostitutes and used marijuana was because he found his job boring and futile. He also claimed that a dispute over his right to use the title of 'Lord' had become an obsession and had led to other obsessions – call girls, marijuana and, bizarrely, gardening!

When Lambton went on television to explain himself he told an interviewer that his actions were just a matter of adding a bit of spice to his life. However, Lambton was minister for the RAF at the time, so the matter was the subject of an official investigation. He was interviewed by MI5, who concluded that there hadn't been a security risk and Lambton vanished into relative obscurity.

Within days of the scandal breaking, another Establishment figure, Lord Jellicoe, also resigned after admitting that he used prostitutes.

Disappearing Act
John Stonehouse

The disappearance of the Labour MP John Stonehouse (1926–88) in 1974 was one of the most bizarre of all political scandals. Stonehouse, the Labour MP for Walsall South, was a minister in Harold Wilson's government in the late 1960s, but found himself out in the cold with no post in the shadow cabinet when the party lost the 1970 election.

Stonehouse had said that his aims were to be a millionaire and become Prime Minister. His political ambitions thwarted, he set about making his fortune. He founded a number of companies, but with little business experience he quickly ran into difficulties. By 1974, his finances were in such a bad way that he conceived an extraordinary plan to escape his financial liabilities. He decided to fake his own death. This would allow him to escape from his financial nightmare, and it would also give him the chance to start a new life in Australia alongside his mistress Sheila Buckley.

Vanishing Act

Buckley was part of the conspiracy and knew what was going on when her lover vanished, along with his real passport and a fake one. Stonehouse travelled to Miami, where he booked into two hotels – one in his own name, the other in the fake name. He then left his clothes on a beach and swam out to sea before carefully swimming back in further up the beach and setting off for his other hotel. However, the plan fell apart when his flight to Australia was delayed. Undaunted, Stonehouse waited a few weeks and executed precisely the same plan again. This time it worked and he took a flight to Australia using his new name.

When the story broke back in England there was a great deal of confusion. The press and MI5 were convinced he'd defected to Russia, but Australian police noticed that Stonehouse's bank accounts began to empty. For some bizarre reason they thought they were on the trail of Lord Lucan, who had also recently disappeared (see pages 110–14). Stonehouse was eventually arrested and deported to Britain in June 1975. He was granted bail while he awaited trial for theft, fraud and deception.

Astonishingly, while on bail Stonehouse continued to take his seat in the House of Commons and even turned up at the Labour Party Conference where he was booed. He then resigned from the Labour Party and joined the English National Party. Stonehouse insisted on conducting his own defence in court, and was sentenced to seven years in prison of which he served five. Sheila Buckley met him on his release and they married in 1981. They lived together until his death eight years later.

That Honours List
Marcia Falkender

When Harold Wilson's (1916–95) infamous resignation honours list was drawn up it did enormous damage to the concept of such awards. The press had a field day, as they mocked the inclusion of various cronies, friends and relations of Marcia Falkender, Wilson's secretary. It became known as the 'Lavender List' as it was drawn up by Falkender on her favourite lavender-coloured paper. The nominees included Joseph Kagan, a coat manufacturer who was later jailed, and even Falkender's sister, who was given an MBE!

We are probably being naïve if we think that honours have ever been properly awarded – Lloyd George and Gladstone sold them by the hundred, as did Charles II, who made his mistresses duchesses and his illegitimate children dukes. However, in Charles II's day there was no pretence that honours and titles should go to anyone other than the favourites of the monarch and his ministers. In the 20th century, we gradually fooled ourselves into thinking that such gongs were deserved. The Lavender List exposed the scandalous truth of the matter.

Even today, arms dealers, failed company directors and major political party donors receive high honours. And seats in the House of Lords often go to politicians, weary of life in the House of Commons, who want somewhere quiet and comfortable to sit, where they can enjoy a good lunch and collect a couple of hundred pounds a day just for turning up.

But back to Marcia Falkender – her real power over Wilson can be judged by a joke that long did the rounds during her tenure at Downing Street. Wilson's press secretary is supposed to have told visitors, 'Marcia can't see you for two weeks but the Prime Minister can see you straight away!'. According to one biographer, Harold Wilson became so concerned about Marcia's ability to control No. 10 that his doctor suggested she should be killed!

Taking Money for Utopia
T. Dan Smith

T. Dan Smith was a Geordie who rose to prominence in the 1960s. From humble beginnings he became leader of Newcastle City Council and was the driving force behind some of the worst modern housing and re-development of the 1960s and 1970s. He was also corrupt and his criminal activities almost brought down a government.

Smith was obsessed with the idea that Newcastle could be a modern vibrant city if only the council would agree to completely rebuild it – he decided that this was a project he would drive through himself come hell or high water. His single-minded determination to bypass all the normal democratic procedures in pursuit of his vision eventually led to a six-year prison term when it was discovered that over the years he'd been paying large sums of money to civil servants, the police and fellow councillors in order to get his way. He'd also accepted bribes from companies eager to get a slice of the re-building programme he'd pushed through and he was the public relations man for his partner in crime – architect John Poulson, who also served time in prison.

The World's Worst Buildings

Smith's Swan House development in the centre of Newcastle has been consistently voted one of the world's most dreadful buildings and it is typical of most of Smith's re-building plans for what had once been an attractive city of mixed architectural styles from various periods. The problem with Smith was that he felt that if other people didn't share his vision then so much the worse for them – he was going to see his Utopia built come what may and, of course, like all Utopias, it was a disaster.

His Cruddas Park housing scheme, for example, was criticized from the moment of its completion – built to a Swedish modular design it alienated those who were meant to live in it and became a haven for gangs, crime and hooliganism. It was far worse than the slums it was meant to replace.

Smith is alleged to have taken bribes during the building of Cruddas Park and indeed for most of the projects which he pushed through. And he could hardly have imagined that within 30 years much of his re-planned city would either be demolished or substantially re-built.

After leaving prison, Smith worked for a number of charities including the Howard League for Prison Reform.

The Eccentric MP
Sir Nicholas Fairbairn

Member of Parliament for Perth, brilliant advocate, painter and much-loved clown, Sir Nicholas Fairbairn (1933–95) was the consummate aristocratic eccentric. His childhood was extremely privileged but troubled, largely because his parents spent most of their time throwing crockery at each other.

Fairbairn studied medicine at Edinburgh, before switching to Classics in order that he might ultimately study for the Bar. He was a terrific showman. For one of his very first cases he turned up wearing an extremely tall hat, which

ABOVE: *Sir Nicholas Fairbairn was a much-loved eccentric.*

he removed in court to reveal a mass of dyed bright-yellow hair. The effect of his curls was set off by an immaculate wing collar, a brightly coloured waist-coat and a silver watch-chain. Having established himself as a successful criminal and divorce lawyer, Fairbairn founded the Society for the Preservation of Duddingston Village, just outside Edinburgh.

He scandalized society by becoming an advocate of birth control long before it was fashionable or even respectable, and once incurred enormous criticism for commenting that rather than send food to African famine victims we should send contraceptives. He entered Parliament in 1974, where he became a great fan of the eventual Prime Minister, Margaret Thatcher, who rewarded him with the job of Solicitor General for Scotland. Fairbairn caused outrage when he commented he thought Thatcher rather sexy, insisting that he was very keen to sleep with her.

He divorced his first wife in 1979, and later married again, designing the Indian-style wedding clothes for himself and his bride. In fact, Fairbairn designed and made all his clothes from the end of the 1980s until his death in February 1995 at the age of 61. However, his sartorial preferences did not appeal to all – one fellow MP described him as looking like a park-keeper.

Fairbairn listed his recreations in *Who's Who* as making love, ends meet and people laugh.

The Politician, the Dog and the Stablelad
Jeremy Thorpe

The scandal of Liberal leader Jeremy Thorpe's fall from grace has more to do with his embarrassment at being gay than anything else. An old Etonian with a taste for expensive clothes, Thorpe (born 1929) was just 37 when he took over the leadership of what was once a great political party, but which by the 1960s had sunk into what seemed like a terminal decline. With the Liberal Party at such a low ebb, Thorpe did at least grab it some attention – only it wasn't quite the attention the party wanted. For almost a decade Thorpe had been lucky – none of his male lovers threatened to expose him – until Norman Scott came on the scene.

Thorpe was born in Surrey. His father was a Conservative MP and the family came from a long line of politicians that stretched back to Mr Speaker Thorpe, who was beheaded by a lynch mob in the late 1300s. During the Blitz, Thorpe was educated in the United States, and on his return to England in 1943 he attended Eton. He managed to escape compulsory National Service after just six weeks and went up to Oxford where he was politically active, becoming president of the Oxford Union in 1951. He was adopted to fight the safe Tory seat of North Devon in 1952, but halved the Tory vote in the 1955 election and scraped home for the Liberals in 1959. His progression through the Liberal Party was rapid – he was a brilliant speaker and fundraiser and did much to further the cause of human rights around the world, so much so that he was banned from entering Spain by Franco.

The Stablelad

By 1969, Thorpe was married. In the 1970 election the Liberals did disastrously and gained only six seats. By the time of the next election, however, he'd revived the party, which gained 14 seats. But in 1975, the scandal that was to destroy Thorpe began to emerge. He had known Norman Scott, a groom, since 1961 and had helped him find work and somewhere to live. From 1966, payments were regularly made to Scott by Thorpe's fellow Liberal MP Peter Bessell. It was all very murky and odd. Scott claimed that he and Thorpe had enjoyed a sexual relationship, which Thorpe denied. A Liberal Party enquiry in 1971 dismissed the Scott allegations, but by the middle of the decade his claims were becoming increasingly outrageous and this is where the real problems began.

It was alleged that, in order to silence Scott, figures close to Thorpe had hired Andrew Newton, an assassin, who drove Scott and his dog Rinka out onto Exmoor. Having stopped the car, Newton then threatened Scott and shot his dog. No one knows whether the gun jammed or Newton had a change of

ABOVE: *JEREMY THORPE WAS ACCUSED OF TRYING TO SILENCE HIS ALLEGED LOVER.*

heart, but Scott was left uninjured.

When, some time later, Scott was tried on an unrelated matter he repeated his allegations against Thorpe. Newton was jailed for the attack and when he was released from prison he claimed he'd been hired to kill Scott. The Liberal MP Peter Bessell then sold his side of the story to a newspaper. Thorpe resigned his leadership and was charged with conspiracy to murder in 1977. The case came to trial in 1979 and he was acquitted, but the judge's summing up made it clear that class bias was involved: he said that he preferred the testimony of a gentleman and an old Etonian to that of a disreputable character such as Scott.

But the Establishment that banded together to save Thorpe from prison was no longer prepared to tolerate such a man in its midst and Thorpe vanished from public life never to be forgiven.

Homes for Votes
Dame Shirley Porter

The Westminster Homes for Votes scandal of the 1980s was particularly shocking because it was the sort of thing we have come to expect only in corruption-ridden African and South American countries.

The basic story was that Shirley Porter, then head of Westminster Council, tried deliberately to sell off council houses in the borough to well-off individuals who could more easily be assumed to be Tory voters than the traditional working-class residents of social housing.

Porter also deliberately tried to move poorer people – assumed Labour voters – out of the borough to change the voting mix in marginal wards in favour of the conservatives. In short, it was a clear-cut case of gerrymandering.

Shirley Porter denied and still denies that she did anything wrong – despite the discovery of internal council documents proving her guilt – but a string of inquiries have been unequivocal in their condemnation of her actions. In December 2001 she took her case to the House of Lords. In giving their judgement the law lords said that her attempts to gain political support by selling off council homes in marginal wards to Tory voters was a 'deliberate, blatant, dishonest misuse of public funds'.

Surcharged to the tune of £27 million, Ms Porter had fled to Israel in the mid-1990s claiming that she was worth only £300,000. However, investigators from Westminster Council discovered she had huge off-shore assets that had found their way into complicated funds and trusts at about the time the surcharge was imposed – it looked suspiciously like a blatant attempt to conceal her wealth from the auditors.

The Tesco Heiress

As she was the heiress to the Tesco superstore empire no one believed her claims of poverty and auditors continued to search for ways to recover the money owed. Estimates of Ms Porter's real wealth varied between a minimum of £69 million and a maximum of £300 million.

By 2003, the High Court had ordered that all traceable assets owned by Shirley Porter or her agents should be frozen – she was also ordered by the court to disclose all her assets including those trusts over which she had power directly or indirectly.

The scandal deepened when an email from Shirley Porter to her son was leaked to the press. It revealed that through a deliberately elaborate series of trusts and intermediates her wealth was still controlled by her or by members of her family.

Amid accusations that Westminster Council was not doing enough to

ABOVE: *The nation publicly mourned when Edward VIII abdicated on the advice of the government which wrongly believed that the king's married, American lover, Wallis Simpson, would not be tolerated.*

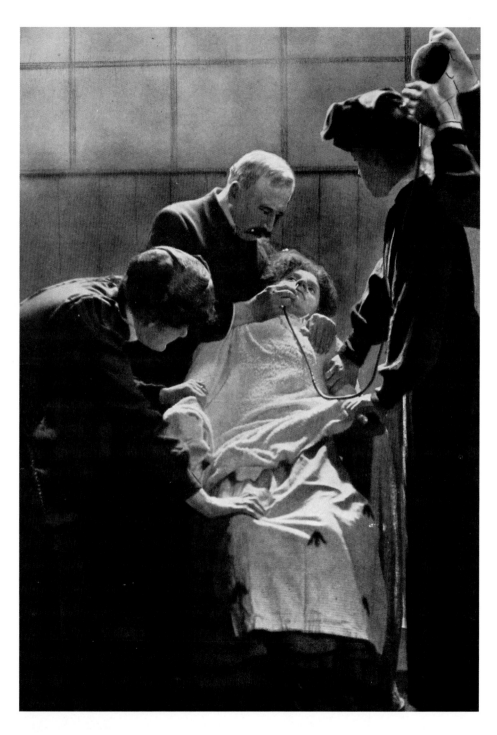

ABOVE: *Force-feeding Suffragettes on hunger strike was abandoned in British prisons due to public outrage at the authorities' barbarism.*

recover the money, it was suggested that Shirley Porter could be found guilty of contempt of court – for lying about her true wealth – and imprisoned, or the council could declare her bankrupt and then try to recover her assets through the bankruptcy courts.

So determined was Shirley Porter to avoid paying her debts that she took Westminster Council to the International Court of Human Rights at Strasbourg. To her great grief, the court rejected her appeal against the £27 million surcharge as 'manifestly ill-founded'. And, with that, her attempts to buy her way out of the corner in which she found herself finally failed and her lawyers agreed a compromise with the council's auditors.

She agreed to pay roughly £12.5 million to the council as a final settlement of the dispute. How she found she was suddenly able to do this when she had claimed earlier that she was worth only £300,000 is a mystery. Westminster Council accepted the offer but have been roundly condemned for not pursuing the full amount.

Perhaps the greatest scandal of the whole sorry saga is that Porter was able to get away with paying only a percentage of what she owed and that no Tory leader has ever condemned what she did while leader of the council, nor have there been moves to strip her of her title.

Shirley Porter will probably never return to the UK. The scandal surrounding her name is simply too great.

Mellor's Mistake
David Mellor

After nearly two decades in power the Conservatives in the 1990s seemed determined to press the self-destruct button. The first half of the decade saw increasingly desperate attempts by John Major to rid his party of its increasingly sleazy image, but the harder he tried, the worse it got. The infamous 'back to basics' campaign, which centred round family values, turned into a disaster as more and more Tory MPs were found to have mistresses, while others were discovered to have strings of undeclared interests in various companies or to have received holidays or other gifts from those with an interest in exerting influence in parliament.

One of the more colourful scandals surrounded the married Heritage Minister David Mellor, who resigned in 1992 after a barrage of tabloid stories about his private life. Mellor had an affair with an actress named Antonia de Sancha, and the main point of the tabloid stories was to ask how the public could trust a man who couldn't be trusted by his wife – if he told her one thing and did another perhaps that's what he also did in his role as a minister and as a constituency MP.

Mellor decided to tough it out and ignore the newspaper calls for him to resign; he even tried to shore up his reputation by posing for pictures with his family – a blatant attempt to create an image that was far from the truth. However, he must have known that when the tabloids have it in for you they never give up. Reporters dug around and quickly discovered that Mellor had taken a free holiday in 1990 as the guest of the daughter of an official of the Palestine Liberation Front. He'd also accepted an all-expenses paid trip from the ruler of Abu Dhabi.

Toe Sucking and Spanking

When Antonia de Sancha spilled the beans to the tabloids, the lurid details probably had more to do with the press trying to spice up the story than with reality. But it was all good stuff – from Mellor's alleged predilection for toe sucking to his passion for spanking. Eventually, Mellor resigned his ministerial post, although he remained MP for Putney until the 1997 election, which saw the almost complete destruction of the Tory party. After he lost his seat, Mellor did some television work and eventually ended up writing a regular column for one of the newspapers that had done so much to destroy his political career.

What was most extraordinary about the Mellor affair was that it was just the first of a long line of similar scandals. Northern Ireland Minister Michael Mates resigned after it was discovered that he'd lobbied parliament on behalf of fugitive businessman Asil Nadir; Tim Yeo was discovered to have fathered an illegitimate child; Alan Duncan resigned after news broke about dodgy dealings concerning a council house and David Ashby left the party after revelations claiming he had shared a bed with a man. The list of Tory misdemeanours seemed almost endless, and it was undoubtedly the biggest cause of the collapse of the party's vote in 1997.

The Man with an Orange in his Mouth
Stephen Milligan

Among the host of sexual scandals that surrounded the last years of the Conservative Government that crashed to defeat in 1997, the story of Stephen Milligan stands out as both bizarre and to some extent inexplicable.

Milligan was considered one of the brightest of the group of younger Tory MPs who won seats in the 1992 General Election. Though his death in 1994 aroused almost universal sympathy it did little to lessen the Tories' increasing reputation for sleaze.

Milligan was just 42 when he died. He had studied at Oxford and became a journalist of some distinction working on the *Times* and the *Economist* before presenting BBC Radio 4's *The World Tonight*. He was secretary of the Conservative Foreign and Commonwealth Council before becoming parliamentary private secretary to Jonathan Aitken then Minister of State for Defence.

Milligan was found dead in the west London house where he lived alone. He was found tied to a chair wearing only stockings and suspenders and with a small orange in his mouth. He also had a plastic bag over his head. Milligan was engaged at the time to a woman who later became an MP and he had no known interest in sado-masochistic sex or in auto-eroticism – unlike his boss Jonathan Aitken, who was said to have rather unorthodox sexual tastes.

No Foul Play

An autopsy decided Milligan had died from asphyxiation caused by an electrical flex found tied tightly round his neck and it was generally accepted that Milligan had got himself into the position in which he was found – that is, after initial short-lived suspicions, the police accepted that there was no evidence of foul play.

It was agreed that this was a bizarre case of auto-eroticism that had somehow gone badly wrong. Whether Milligan had tied himself up too tightly or slipped in some way and inadvertently tightened the noose will never be known, but those with experience in this area say that the feeling of bondage and restriction can be enormously arousing. The effects are said to be not unlike those used in medieval brothels to arouse elderly or impotent customers. They were throttled for a while as this tended to produce an erection. In Milligan's case the throttling was too much and he clearly lost consciousness before he could loosen his bonds. This may be borne out by the fact that the forensic team removed parts of a cupboard from the house. If Milligan had tied himself to something immovable and then slipped, a noose round his neck would quickly have hanged him.

No alcohol or drugs were found in the body and the coroner's verdict was death by misadventure. It was a bizarre scandal and one that to this day leaves many questions unanswered. What made it particularly awkward for the Tory government was that it made a large section of 'respectable' middle-class, middle-income Britain very suspicious of pin-stripe wearing right-wing MPs!

Brown Paper Bags
Neil Hamilton

Neil Hamilton is perhaps the best-known exponent of the art of digging yourself into a hole and then refusing to stop digging. As a barrister he was clearly convinced that the law could be made to do what he wanted it to do, so when he was accused of accepting cash to ask questions in parliament he refused to go quietly. The 'cash for questions' accusations were made by Mohammed Al Fayed, the owner of Harrods, who was furious that he could not persuade the government to give him a British passport, despite spending huge amounts of money cultivating various MPs.

Hamilton entered parliament in 1983 as the Tory MP for Tatton in Cheshire. He was tipped for a role in government and was eventually promoted to government whip and Minister of Corporate Affairs. In the 1990s, rumours spread that he had accepted regular gifts of cash – delivered, it was said, in brown paper bags – in return for asking questions in parliament. Hamilton denied the charges, which were widely discussed in the media. But, coming at the end of a long line of similarly sleazy accusations against John Major's increasingly beleaguered government, the scandal was largely to blame for Hamilton being ousted from his Tatton seat in the 1997 election. His seat was taken by an independent candidate – the former BBC journalist, Martin Bell – who stood on an anti-sleaze ticket.

Tory Scapegoat

Hamilton was blamed – rightly or wrongly – for the Conservatives' landslide defeat. He became something of a scapegoat for all that was wrong with the party, which suffered its worst election defeat in history. By 1998, Hamilton was even being asked to keep away from the Tory Party Conference – William Hague, the party's then leader, publicly condemned him for bringing the Conservatives into disrepute.

By this time, Hamilton was engaged in a libel action against The *Guardian* newspaper, but he dropped it on the eve of his courtroom appearance. Having dropped this action you would think that he would have realized that his reputation was in tatters and that further action in the courts was likely to make things worse not better, but Hamilton refused to give up and sued Al Fayed – and lost.

The action was a direct response to accusations made on television that Hamilton had accepted gifts of cash and a holiday from the Harrods boss. The result of the trial was probably a foregone conclusion, but the press had a field day with the eccentric replies given by Al Fayed to questions from Hamilton's council. Al Fayed said he spent as much as £120,000 in cash a week, all of it legitimately. When Desmond Browne QC queried this, Al Fayed lost his temper:

'You have nothing to defend your client except attacking me unfairly, unlogically because you don't understand what type of person I am, what culture I come from, what commitments I have, how many people I employ.'

ABOVE: *Neil Hamilton and his loyal wife Christine have forged careers as c-list celebrities following their high-profile – and disastrous – court case.*

As the questioning continued he could barely contain himself:

'You have no basis for all this rubbish. You are just trying to ridicule me. I have a lot of commitments, big family, homes everywhere. I need the cash and it's none of your business. My personal cash is my personal life. It's none of your bloody business. It's my business. Get on with the subject and don't waste the time of everybody.'

How the Mighty Have Fallen
Jonathan Aitken

People probably only ever said that Jonathan Aitken, born in 1942, had potential because he had the sort of background the English can't help admire. He was good looking, a bit of a cad, snootily elegant, had been to Eton and Oxford and his father was the 1st Baron Rugby; he was also incredibly arrogant. Much as we may have disliked him for this, it was impossible not to admire – however begrudgingly – a man who had enough money and influence to do and say whatever he liked.

In predictable fashion he became a Tory MP in 1974 and then a cabinet minister. Mrs Thatcher thought he was wonderful until he unceremoniously dumped her daughter Carole with whom he'd had a long-term relationship. Mrs Thatcher then dumped Aitken. By 1992, after Thatcher's removal from power, he was back in favour and became Minister of State for Defence Procurement under John Major. By 1994, he was Chief Secretary to the Treasury; by 1995, he was in trouble.

Putting on the Ritz

He was accused by the *Guardian* newspaper and Granada TV of having stayed in the Ritz Hotel in Paris at the expense of an Arab arms dealer – something strictly forbidden under the rules governing the behaviour of ministers. As Aitken was Minister for Defence Procurement the matter was especially sensitive and potentially scandalous.

In order to clear his name, Aitken sued both Granada TV and the *Guardian* and made grandiose claims about his aims that were to come back and haunt him. Most famously, he told the press that in his battle with the media he would use 'the simple sword of truth and the trusty shield of fair play'. The trial collapsed in June 1997 after he'd lost his seat in the General Election that swept Labour to power with a huge majority.

Aitken was proved a liar by sensational written evidence, obtained by the *Guardian*. This evidence proved that Aitken's wife's claim that she had paid for her husband's stay at the Ritz could not possibly be true, as they had procured a copy of the bill from the hotel marked 'debiteur M Ayas'. Ayas was the Arab businessman accused of having paid Aitken's bill.

The bill had been shown to the then editor of the *Guardian*, Peter Preston, by a disgruntled Mohammed Al Fayed, owner of both the Paris Ritz and top people's store Harrods. Al Fayed had taken a dislike to the Tory government for refusing to grant him a British passport. The *Guardian* began an investigation that exposed various arms scams involving Aitken's friend Said Ayas – the same Ayas who'd paid that hotel bill.

What made things far worse for Aitken was that following the collapse of the trial it emerged that he had planned to get his daughter Victoria to sign an affadavit supporting his lies about who paid the hotel bill. Charged with perjury and perverting the course of justice, Aitken was jailed in 1999 for 18 months and released after just seven months. He was declared bankrupt – his fabulously expensive house in Lord North Street, Westminster, having been transferred, curiously enough, to his now ex-wife.

Aitken resigned from the Privy Council – one of only three people to do so in more than a century – and, despite expressing a desire to re-enter politics, has now accepted that his political career is over.

Unlike many bankrupts, Aitken did not find himself friendless and poverty stricken when he left prison. Rather than go and live in social housing in the darker depths of south London, he returned to his old Oxford College to study theology and remarried in 2003.

Mr Toad takes his Todger out
Alan Clark

Alan Clark, whose diaries caused a minor sensation when they were first published in the late 1990s, was a maverick Tory minister who adored Mrs Thatcher to the point of obsequiousness. He knew he would never be appointed to one of the great offices of state, despite his conviction that he knew better than anyone how the country ought to be run, but worried and fretted endlessly that even in his relatively lowly position he would not live up to Mrs Thatcher's expectations.

Enormously wealthy, Clark was the son of Kenneth Clark the historian whose BBC's televison series *Civilisation* made him a household name in the 1960s. Father and son seem to have got on very badly and Clark seems to have inherited many of his father's less attractive qualities – even the younger Clark's friends – including several fellow Tory MPs – admitted that Clark was a bully who enjoyed being unpleasant to those who worked for him.

But while a Tory MP, Clark's real aim was to write and then publish his diaries – diaries that he hoped would make him a modern-day Pepys. To some extent this ambition was fulfilled as the 'Diaries' did indeed sell very well, but not so much because they revealed anything useful about how the Tory government and the personalities within it worked. What really appealed was that Clark's diaries were filled with the tittle-tattle and bitter schoolboy envies of high office. Better still, Clark revealed his own personality – he comes across as a sort of Mr Toad without the endearing qualities.

What the newspapers and reviewers really enjoyed, however, was the fact that Clark admitted he knew that the whole family values nonsense pushed endlessly by the Tories was bunkum. Without embarrassment, Clark confessed to having had sex with a woman he did not know on a train to London. He also confessed that he had seduced and had simultaneous affairs with judge's wife Valerie Harkness and her two daughters Josephine and Alison.

Perhaps most infamous of all was the fact that Clark numbered among his best friends disgraced minister Jonathan Aitken (see above).

Curried Major
John Major and Edwina Currie

The most delightful thing about the scandal involving John Major and Edwina Currie is that we now know that all the time the Tories were encouraging a 'back to basics' attitude to morality, members of the party from the top down were carrying on as usual with extra-marital affairs. Somehow, Major's reputation as a decent bloke made the revelations that bit more disreputable, but it was clear that Currie had kept a lid on the relationship in order to spice up her memoirs, which is where the story first emerged.

Currie's memoirs were published in 2003, but it is remarkable that no hint of the affair reached the press while it was actually going on. Prime Ministers hardly get a minute's privacy so, how on earth, asked journalists and commentators, did the sly old devil get away with it – and, having got away with it, how did the story remain hidden for so long?

After the affair became public, Major couldn't put a foot right. The relationship had allegedly lasted four years and ended two years before he took office as Prime Minister. Confronted with the truth, Major, rather than remain silent, stated that it was the event in his life of which he was most ashamed. This prompted the inevitable response from Currie who stated that he hadn't seemed ashamed at the time.

The Longest 'Event' in History

Edwina Currie probably comes out of the affair best, given that at any time during Major's four-year premiership she could have made untold thousands from the tabloids by telling her story. The scandal would undoubtedly have brought the Major government down far earlier than the election of 1997. It also seems odd that Major described the affair as an 'event' – four years is hardly an event in anyone's language.

Currie was never one to avoid controversy. After studying at Oxford she lectured at the Open University before becoming a local councillor in 1975. In 1983, she became an MP and then in 1986 became a minister at the Department of Health and Social Services. She courted scandal by criticizing the eating habits of Northeners as unhealthy, and then appeared on television demonstrating the use of a condom. However, her biggest mistake was to say that most of Britain's eggs were infected with salmonella. The storm that erupted after this forced her to resign as a minister.

Like so many Tory MPs, Currie lost her seat in 1997, and has since carved out a career as a writer of bodice rippers – one can only assume that many of the steamy sex sessions described in her books are based on her own experiences.

What is ironic is that Major always appeared to be the archetypal grey bureaucrat. The revelations of his raunchy sex sessions with Currie have transformed him into a jack-the-lad figure, whose own autobiography is now eagerly awaited by the scandal-loving public.

Outrageous Royals –
Kinky Kings and Pouting Princesses

'The important thing is not what they think of me, but what I think of them.'

Queen Victoria

Death by Red-hot Poker
Edward II

History has not been kind to Edward II (1307–27), who is perceived as one of England's weakest monarchs. His father Edward I (1272–1307) detested his son's addiction to what were perceived as unmanly pursuits – the worst of which was gardening. In desperation, the king imported a young man named Piers Gaveston (1284–1312) from France who, it was hoped, would encourage the young Prince of Wales to take part in jousting, hunting and other more masculine pursuits. Unfortunately, the plan backfired on a major scale and precipitated the biggest royal scandal of the Middle Ages – the young Edward fell passionately in love with the Frenchman, a sentiment that was evidently reciprocated.

A contemporary noted that 'when the king's son saw him he fell so much in love that he entered upon an enduring compact with him and chose and determined to knit an indissoluble bond with him.' In plainer terms, they were absolutely mad about each other. Edward I was warlike, violent and ill-tempered – all the things a manly medieval king should have been. He quickly realized his mistake and tried to keep Gaveston and his son apart, but with little success.

Both Loved and Hated

Soon, the besotted prince was showering gifts on Gaveston, who became the most hated figure at court – he was arrogant and insensitive to the established courtiers who surrounded the royal family – but nothing could be done about Gaveston while he enjoyed the favour of the Prince of Wales. However, the prince over-reached himself when he asked his father to make his companion an earl. The king was furious and, in front of the court, he grabbed his son by the hair and pulled him around until a great chunk of it fell out.

Edward I banished Gaveston from England in 1307. However, when the king died in July of that year, Edward II, as he now was, recalled his lover immediately and made him Duke of Cornwall. Gaveston then married Edward's niece and began to assume more of the duties normally assigned to English nobles. Resentment grew again though when the extent of Gaveston's spending from the royal coffers became clear.

By this time, some courtiers had begun to think that Gaveston had unearthly powers – one contemporary chronicler described him as 'a sorcerer' – and this can only have been confirmed by his being made regent while the king travelled to Boulogne to collect his young bride, Isabella of France (1294–1358). All the time, hatred and resentment for Gaveston grew. When the king returned to England he was greeted by Gaveston, who was so weighed

down with diamonds, rubies and other jewels that he could hardly walk. Gaveston even insisted on organizing Edward's coronation. It was a disaster – there was insufficient room for all the nobles attending (one person even died in the crush) and the food was inedible.

When the new queen wrote to her father saying that Edward was a stranger to her bed, the English nobles felt they had to act. Using threats and entreaties they persuaded Edward that Gaveston had to go for the sake of the kingdom. He was stripped of his titles and sent packing. The Church was persuaded to pronounce a sentence of excommunication on Gaveston should he ever return to England, but he petitioned the Pope successfully. Once again, Gaveston returned to Edward. By now, the English bishops and nobles were so outraged they took over the king's finances and prepared for war. Gaveston and Edward fled to Scotland where they split up and the king made an unsuccessful attempt to raise an army. But the game was up – Gaveston was captured and beheaded in 1312. Edward was inconsolable, although he cheered slightly when his wife gave birth to the future Edward III shortly afterwards.

The Revenge of the She-Wolf

Edward's reign remained unstable, with various noble factions squabbling about how England should be ruled. In 1325, a discontented Isabella travelled to France, followed shortly afterwards by her son. In 1326, Isabella, the She-Wolf of France, as she became known, invaded England with her son and her lover Roger De Mortimer (1287–1330). Edward escaped towards the West Country, but was captured and forced to abdicate in 1327. He was locked up in Berkeley Castle, where he was kept in the most appalling conditions and eventually murdered. Rumour has it that a red-hot poker was pushed into his backside in order to kill him without leaving a mark on his body!

Betrothals and Beheadings
Henry VIII

Catholics are fond of telling Anglicans that their church was founded by a psychopathic dictator who made himself Keeper of the Faith for the sole purpose of divorcing his wives and enriching himself. Of course, that is a partial reading of history, but it is ironic that the family values espoused by today's Anglican clergy sit oddly with the man who founded it – a man who spent his life disposing of women who failed to bear him a son.

It may not be entirely fair to judge Henry VIII (1509–47) by the standards of another age, but even in his own time his behaviour was roundly condemned by large sections of the population. They saw it as extraordinary that one man could overturn a thousand years of Christian history to suit his own ends. Those who refused to accept that the king was head of the Church, including his one time friend and confidant Sir Thomas More (1475–1535), were brutally executed.

The 1536 Pilgrimage of Grace showed just how horrified the people were at Henry's behaviour. The pilgrimage brought together more than 30,000 people, mostly from the north. They marched on London to protest at the treatment being meted out to monks during Henry's Dissolution of the Monasteries. Henry's armies could not have defeated the huge numbers involved in the protest, so he met the leaders and agreed to discuss their grievances. As soon as the marchers dispersed, Henry had the leaders

LEFT: *Henry VIII*
HAD SIX WIVES IN TOTAL, TWO OF WHICH HE HAD BEHEADED.

rounded up and executed. Robert Aske, who had organized the pilgrimage, was burned at the stake.

The Six Wives

There is no doubt that Henry was obsessed with the idea of ensuring the Tudor succession. When argument failed to persuade Pope Clement to annul Henry's first marriage to Katherine of Aragon (1485–1536) the king was furious, largely because he believed that the decision taken against him in Rome had more to do with politics than religion. This was a reasonable view given that the Pope was linked to Charles V who was both Holy Roman Emperor and Katherine's nephew.

Before his break with Rome and divorce in 1533, which was never legal in the eyes of the Catholic church, Henry was already involved with his next wife, Anne Boleyn (1507–36), the mother of the future Elizabeth I. Henry married Anne in 1533, but executed her on trumped up charges of infidelity in May 1536. Very shortly after his second wife's death, Henry married Jane Seymour (1509–37) who died giving birth to Henry's longed-for heir, Edward, in October 1537. In 1540, he married Anne of Cleves (1515–57), but found her so physically repellent that he divorced her in the same year and married Katherine Howard (1521–42) who was also executed for infidelity – as in the case of Anne Boleyn the charges were somewhat spurious. Henry finally married Catherine Parr (1512–48) in 1543. She probably only survived because Henry himself died in 1547.

It is ironic that Henry's ferocious hold on power ultimately led to the execution of Charles I (1625–49) a century later. By then, parliament was fed up with monarchs who felt they could do just as they pleased – which is precisely what Henry had always done.

Lovers of the Scottish Queen
Mary, Queen of Scots

It was political intrigue that finally led to the execution of Mary, Queen of Scots (1542–67) in 1587, although her private life might easily have been enough to condemn her. Mary was the second daughter of James V of Scotland who died when she was just a week old. Before she left the nursery Henry VIII went to great lengths to ensure that she was betrothed to his son, Edward, his ultimate aim being to gain English control over Scotland.

When the Scottish parliament annulled the engagement, Henry used it as an excuse to declare war. The Scots were defeated at the Battle of Pinkie in

1547 and Mary left for France, where she grew up at the court of the French ruler Henry II. In 1558, she married the Dauphin, Francis. He died in 1560 when Mary was just 18. She returned to Scotland in 1561 to find that the Protestant lords who had been running the country had tried to ban the authority of the pope. Mary, an ardent Catholic, insisted on celebrating mass at Holyrood Palace, an action that provoked a riot.

An Unwanted Husband

In 1565, Mary married her handsome cousin Henry Stuart, Lord Darnley (1545–67). However, she fell out with him quickly, amid rumours of his drunkenness and depraved sexual appetites. Darnley was also involved in a conspiracy that led to the murder of Mary's companion and possible lover, David Rizzio. In 1566, Mary gave birth to the future James VI, who also became the English king in 1603. She was never reconciled with Darnley, who was killed in mysterious circumstances in 1567 – he was injured in an explosion that should have killed him, and then found strangled in the grounds of his house. It is likely that Mary was involved in the murder, but it has never been proven. However, the events of the months that followed cast a shadow of guilt over her that has never been dispelled.

In the immediate aftermath of Darnley's death, the Earl of Bothwell (1536–78), a close friend of the queen's, was accused of the murder, but he was acquitted after a farcical trial that was never likely to have convicted him. Mary was then kidnapped – probably willingly – by Bothwell. She made him Duke of Orkney and married him. By this time, tongues – to put it mildly – were wagging. It was a Scottish scandal on an unprecedented scale.

Scotland's nobles immediately rose against Mary, and she was forced to abdicate. The marriage had given the Protestant lords just the excuse they needed to get rid of the Catholic queen they despised. Mary escaped and raised an army, but she was defeated at Langside in 1568. Hoping for the protection of her cousin, Elizabeth I (1533–1603), she escaped to England, but was there imprisoned. She remained under lock and key until Elizabeth, increasingly irritated by her presence and fearful that she was plotting to seize the English throne, signed the warrant for her execution in 1587.

A Mistress in Every Cupboard
Charles II

Charles II (1660–85) loved pleasure, it was not for nothing that he was known as the Merry Monarch. He adored masques and balls, plays, drinking, eating and

– best of all – women. He was married to Catherine of Braganza (1638–1705), of whom he was fond, although she failed to produce an heir. However, Charles had numerous children by more than a dozen mistresses. In addition to his long-standing lovers, it is certain that he had numerous brief liaisons with actresses, servants and other men's wives, most of whom didn't mind a bit.

This sort of behaviour wasn't seen as scandalous by the standards of the Restoration court, largely because many of the courtiers behaved in precisely the same way. Outside the court, however, it was a different story and the older puritans who had run the country during the Commonwealth were appalled by Charles's behaviour. Many believed that the decadence of the court, which was positively encouraged by the king, was some sort of sign that the world was soon to come to an end – it was as if sin would reach a peak just before Christ's second coming.

When Charles II first returned from exile in France in 1660 to take the throne he executed a number of those who had signed the death warrant of his father, Charles I. However, he didn't make his father's mistake of ruling as an absolute monarch. His energy was directed in an entirely different direction. Knowing the sensitivities of parliament, the king was careful not to alienate his nobles, but this wasn't difficult as he had very little interest in work anyway. He was keen that there should be religious tolerance – hardly surprising as he attended mass during his lifetime, disliked the prevalent anti-Catholic feeling in the country and converted to Rome on his deathbed.

Public Pleasures

Charles was popular with his subjects as he refused to promote the sort of restrictions on pleasure that the previous regime had introduced. During the reign of the Puritans, the theatres had been closed. Charles, on the other hand, actively encouraged them, and also insisted that women were allowed to act – something that outraged the more conservative elements of society. He also supported playwrights such as William Congreve and William Wycherley, who wrote amoral comedies that featured themes such as seduction and cuckolding and in which the villain of the piece usually got away with his crimes. No other king protected and promoted so many rakes and libertines. He was even amused when the Earl of Rochester (see pages 14–17) wrote 'A Satyr on Charles II':

> His sceptre and his prick are of a length;
> And she may sway the one who plays with th'other,
> And make him little wiser than his brother.
> Poor prince! they prick, like thy buffoons at Court,
> Will govern thee because it makes thee sport.
> 'Tis sure the sauciest prick that e'er did swive,
> The proudest, peremptoriest prick alive.
> Though safety, law, religion, life lay on't,
> 'Twould break through all to make its way to cunt.
> Restless he rolls about from whore to whore,
> A merry monarch, scandalous and poor.

Only one woman is known to have refused to sleep with Charles – Frances Stuart, one of the great beauties of the age. Whether it was the general freedom encouraged by Charles or some other influence, Frances liked to dress up in men's clothing. At one point, she went through a mock marriage with one of Charles' mistresses, Barbara Palmer while dressed as a man. At the time of the 'ceremony' Palmer was pregnant with Charles's child. After the marriage the two women went to bed together and apparently invited Charles in to watch!

'The Nation's Best-Loved Whore'
Nell Gwyn

'A brazen wanton' was how one contemporary puritan described Nell Gwyn (1650–87), one of Charles II's many mistresses. But despite, or perhaps because of, her scandalous life she was much loved by the London populace and became a legend in her own lifetime. This had much to do with her racy wit,

> **'Pray good people be civil. I am the protestant whore.'**
>
> Nell Gwyn

generosity, good temper and complete lack of airs and graces. When her carriage was being jostled by the mob because they thought she was Louise de Keroualle (1649–1734) the king's French – and therefore Catholic – mistress she shouted through the window: 'Pray good people be civil. I am the protestant whore.'

When a courtier tried to persuade Nell to sleep with him after she'd become Charles's mistress she said, 'I shall not lay a dog where a deer has lain!' Despite being short and not particularly beautiful, Nell never lost the affection of Charles. She was his mistress from 1670 until his death in 1685. On his deathbed he instructed his brother, who was to become James II, 'Let not poor Nelly starve'. Unlike his other 13 mistresses, Nell never pressed Charles for honours, although he did award her a generous pension. However, she did persuade him to ennoble their son.

On a visit to Nell in her house in Lincoln's Inn Fields to see his son, Charles encountered the little boy playing on the far side of the room.

'Come here you little bastard, and speak to your father,' shouted Nell.

The king was horrified. 'Nay, Nelly do not give the child such a name.'

'Your majesty hath given me no other name by which I may call him,' she replied.

The king promptly gave the boy the name Charles Beauclerk (1670–1726) and created him Earl of Burford. In 1684, Charles was made Duke of St Albans.

Orange Seller and Actress

Nell Gwyn was born in either Hereford or London, there is no hard evidence either way. She was illiterate, scrawling her initials at the end of letters that were written for her by others once she had become rich through the king's patronage. She was red-haired, fiery and amusing. Legend has it that as a child she sold oranges outside the Covent Garden theatre. She was quickly noticed by the actor Charles Hart and became his mistress. By the age of 15, Nell was appearing regularly on the stage and her appearance in John Dryden's *Secret Love* in 1667 was greeted rapturously by at least one member of the audience. The diarist Samuel Pepys (see pages 146–7) wrote 'so great a performance of a comical part was never, I believe, in the world before… so done by Nell her merry part as cannot be better done in nature.' Her reputation spread and she became the most admired and loved actress of her day. Dryden wrote a number of parts specifically for her, but when she became the king's mistress in 1670 her acting career came to an end.

She benefited enormously from being Charles's lover, but unlike his other mistresses was never seen as avaricious – another facet of her character that endeared her to Londoners. Nell knew that the best way to please the king was not to beg for money and honours – it was to satisfy him in bed. It was advice given to her by her contemporary, the poet John Wilmot (see pages 14–15), who wrote this typically bawdy verse.

> This you'd believe, had I but time to tell ye,
> The pains it costs to poor, laborious Nelly,
> Whilst she employs hands, fingers, mouth, and thighs
> Ere she can raise the member she enjoys

Having lived in luxury, Nell built up huge debts. At one stage imprisonment was on the cards, but James remembered his brother's injunction to help her and paid what she owed. Nell survived the king by just three years and was buried in St Martin-in-the-Fields, Westminster.

A Marriage of Convenience
George IV and Queen Caroline

When George IV (1820–30) turned up at Westminster Abbey for his coronation in 1820, he scandalized the nation by arranging for officials to shut the doors in his wife's face when she arrived to see her husband crowned. It was one of the last in a series of widely publicized incidents in the lives of an extremely unhappy royal couple.

George IV was the eldest son of the happy couple George III and Charlotte of Mecklenberg-Streliotz. He never really escaped from the shadow of his father who suffered from increasingly lengthy bouts of insanity, caused by porphyria. Father and son disliked each other intensely and the younger George seems to have inherited something of his father's instability. In 1795, he married his cousin, Caroline of Brunswick (1768–1821), solely to keep Parliament happy. However, the marriage was effectively bigamous – George was already married! He had conceived a passion for Maria Fitzherbert (1756–1837) who refused to become his mistress, and so he married her in a secret ceremony in 1785. To add to the scandal, Maria was a Catholic – although this did mean that under the Royal Marriages Act, the union was illegal.

Unhappily Married

The prince's marriage to Caroline was purely one of convenience. He wanted Parliament to pay off the huge debts that he had accumulated through gambling, drinking and womanizing. The only way to do it was to marry a Protestant. From the instant they met, Caroline and George loathed each other. Evidence from surviving correspondence suggests that somehow they managed to have sex three times. One of these occasions produced a daughter, Charlotte Augusta. The couple never lived together – George complained that she was unhygienic and that she had not been a virgin when he married her. She, in turn, complained that George was fat and rude.

Eventually, Caroline retired to a house in Blackheath and indulged herself with a string of lovers before leaving England. She became famous for spending money and for outrageous parties. However, when George was crowned in 1820, Caroline decided to return to England to claim her rightful place as queen. George was aghast at the prospect and persuaded parliament to bring in an act allowing him to divorce. But the new king – by now vastly overweight and addicted to alcohol and laudanum – was extremely unpopular and there were demonstrations against him and his plans to divorce. The row continued to simmer and only came to an end when Caroline died suddenly in 1821.

By now, drugs and alcohol had taken their toll and, like his father, George IV was showing signs of madness. He became something of a recluse and when he did appear he insisted he'd been the hero of the Battle of Waterloo. He died in 1830 at Windsor.

A Scandalous Passion
Queen Victoria and John Brown

In many ways, the close relationship between Queen Victoria (1837–1901) and John Brown (1826–83) helped to create the image of the loyal but proud Highland ghillie. Although he was a servant, Brown was treated with enormous respect and affection by Victoria. So much so that she insisted – to the outrage of some people – that his photograph should be buried with her.

The Faithful Servant

Brown, who was born on a farm at Craithie, was already working at Balmoral when Queen Victoria and Prince Albert bought the estate in 1847. He started as an assistant, working his way up the ranks to become Albert's favourite ghillie. When Albert died in 1861 and Victoria retreated in mourning to Scotland, Brown became ever closer to the queen. To the scandal of the court, he treated her as if she were an ordinary mortal, openly criticizing her and indulging in banter with her.

Some courtiers grew to dislike Brown intensely, partly because they felt that it was inappropriate that a commoner should be so close to the queen and partly out of pure jealously that they were not treated in the same way. As the friendship grew, courtiers tried to give the impression that gossip about her relationship with Brown was damaging Victoria's reputation, but it made no difference, particularly after Brown disarmed a would-be assailant, rescuing the queen from injury and possibly even death.

Rumours were deliberately spread about Brown in an attempt to blacken his name. Yet, it did no good. Victoria dismissed them as malicious gossip and gave Brown two awards that she created just for him – the Faithful Servant Medal and the Devoted Service Medal. She also awarded him an annuity and commissioned a life-sized portrait and statue of her favourite. The relief at court when Brown died at the age of just 56 must have been palpable, but Victoria never forgot him.

Victoria's son Edward, later Edward VII (see below), loathed the ghillie, and when his mother died he destroyed almost everything that had anything to do with Brown. Curiously, however, he did not have Brown's statue destroyed, although it was moved into an obscure corner of the estate at Balmoral where it remains to this day.

Multiple Mistresses
Edward VII

Harshly treated by his mother, Queen Victoria, Edward VII (1901–1910) let go of the reins entirely when she finally died in 1901. The pious, serious son she had hoped to create by telling him how hopeless he was in comparison to her late husband, had turned into an overweight sensualist who enjoyed the favours of a string of mistresses. He spent his relatively short time as king indulging his passion for eating, drinking, shooting and, of course, women.

But with all this there was a difficulty. No whiff of scandal was allowed to attach itself to the King of England, so, despite the vast hypocrisy of the situation, elaborate efforts were made by the king's courtiers to make sure he could do as he pleased while appearing to stick to the rules of decorum and good behaviour. For example, the 200-year old Covent Garden restaurant, Rules, built a special side door, which led to a private room where Edward entertained his mistresses, and when he went to the theatre he was ushered into a private box well away from the public gaze.

Much of this is, of course, well known, but less well known is Edward's passion for fire engines, which led to some very odd behaviour at No. 13 Rupert Street in Soho. Here, Edward would enter as king and emerge on top of a fire engine disguised as a fireman. No one knows quite how often he indulged this fancy, but the best estimate is that it went on for most of his reign.

My Kingdom for a Wife
Edward VIII and Mrs Simpson

It was arguably the greatest royal scandal of the 20th or any century. In a solemn radio announcement, broadcast to the nation, the King of England, Edward VIII (1936) renounced his throne in order to marry a woman who was both divorced and – possibly worse – American.

It was 1936 and the Establishment was outraged by these momentous events. The general public, by contrast, was enormously sympathetic. The Abdication Crisis was seen as intensely romantic, and it somehow fitted the image of an unconventional monarch who had spent much of his adult life trying to escape the traditionally aloof world of royal protocol. The king's desire to be close to his people – his desire somehow to be different – probably had its roots in an unhappy childhood and adolescence, but the relaxed and informal manner he adopted with ordinary people was seen as inappropriate by his advisors. They felt that the king, by definition, should be remote from the people.

Edward Albert Christian George Andrew Patrick David Windsor was born in 1894 to the Duke and Duchess of York, later King George V and Queen Mary. His parents were apparently emotionally cold and completely undemonstrative. They seemed to pay attention to their son only when they wanted to punish him for some misdeed or other.

Edward, who had four brothers and a sister, was sent to the Royal Naval College on the Isle of Wight in 1907, where he seems to have made enormous efforts to avoid being treated in any way that marked him out from the other students. While at Dartmouth Naval College in 1910, he heard the news that his grandfather, Edward VII, had died. His father became George V and Edward was now heir to the throne.

In 1911, Edward became Prince of Wales and hated the archaic uniform he was forced to wear at his investiture. When war was declared in 1914, he joined up and immediately asked to be sent to the front line. Lord Kitchener refused his request, not on the grounds that Edward might be killed, but that he might be captured and somehow put on display by the enemy. However, Edward's request was common knowledge and his popularity among the ordinary soldiers increased as a result. As it turned out, he ended up well away from the front, working for Sir John French, the Commander-in-Chief of the British Expeditionary Force.

The Prince's Preferences

After the war, the prince settled into the life of a typical royal, but the whiff of scandal soon began to attach itself to the future king – it was noted that he was always attracted to married women. In 1918, he met Mrs Winifred Dudley Ward a married woman with whom he went on to conduct a 16-year affair.

Royalty and the aristocracy simply paid lip service to the rules laid down by Church and State and did, as they had done for centuries, exactly as they pleased. They knew that in the climate of intense deference that existed at the time no newspaper would dare publish a word about the private life of a prince.

Thus, in tandem with his relationship with Mrs Ward, Edward enjoyed a number of liaisons with other women. He was good looking and, legend has it, sexually inexhaustible. On January 10, 1931, at a party at the house of Viscountess Thelma Furness, another of his mistresses, the prince met the woman who was to change his life forever.

Wallis Simpson arrived at the party with her husband Ernest. She was introduced to the prince, and onlookers thought that the two had taken something of a dislike to each other. However, a few weeks later Edward had dinner with Mr and Mrs Simpson at their house. From then on, the frequency with which Edward and Mrs Simpson met increased dramatically. Mrs Simpson accepted numerous invitations to join the prince and their relationship soon became sexual, although Edward continued to enjoy the favours of a number of other women.

The Captivating Mrs Simpson

Mrs Simpson's growing influence over Edward can be judged by the fact that from 1934 onwards his other mistresses – Mrs Ward and Viscountess Furness among them – were ostracized by the prince. Their telephone calls were not returned and they no longer received invitations to parties and dances. It was as if they had ceased to exist. On the face of it, Mrs Simpson did not seem to be the sort of person likely to captivate the prince quite as completely as she did. Indeed, historians still puzzle about how she came to exert such a hold over him.

ABOVE: *Mrs Simpson wasn't the first married woman to catch Prince Edward's eye.*

She was born Wallis Warfield on 19 June, 1896 in Maryland. She grew up with an easy, friendly manner, was generally agreed to be amusing, but was by no means considered a beauty. In 1916, she married Lieutenant Earl Winfield Spencer, a US Navy pilot. Wallis left him when he began drinking, but rejoined him when he was posted to China. They were eventually divorced in 1927. Six months later she married Ernest Simpson, who worked for his family's shipping business. The couple decided to live in London where they were invited into society.

When George V died on 20 January, 1936 it was clear that Edward, now king, was completely infatuated by Mrs Simpson – that at least was the view of those who knew him well at the time. What was also clear was that nothing was going to make him give her up. In many ways Edward disliked his new role and the eminence it brought – something that, with hindsight, makes it easier to understand his decision to renounce it.

One of his first acts on his accession was to dismiss the advisers he inherited from his father. He also began to modernize the monarchy – a task that outraged the court. He cut the salaries of royal staff, avoided protocol and frequently ignored the boxes of official papers sent to him – he muddled them up, failed to return them or sent them back without having even glanced at them. He constantly cancelled official duties in order to be with his lover, and, despite the deference paid to him, the scandal began to grow and became increasingly difficult to control. Mistresses were allowed, even in large numbers, but not if they appeared to dominate the king.

Constitutional Crisis

The scandal threatened to break into the public domain when Alexander Hardinge, the king's private secretary, wrote to Edward warning him that the government might resign if the situation did not improve and that they would certainly resign if the press mentioned what was going on.

Edward had three options. He could give up Mrs Simpson; he could remain king and accept the resignation of the government and the ensuing constitutional crisis or he could abdicate. The Prime Minister, Stanley Baldwin, told Edward that the people would not accept his marriage to a divorced woman and in many ways this – an outright lie – was as outrageous as the king's obsession. All the evidence suggests that the people would indeed have accepted Mrs Simpson, so long as she was his morganatic wife – that is, she did not herself become queen. It was the Establishment's dislike and manipulation of the matter that led to an ultimatum: Edward would have to give up Mrs Simpson or abdicate. In fact, as king, he could have refused to abdicate and insisted on marrying Mrs Simpson whatever the consequences. He would have been entitled to do this in the same way that monarchs in previous centuries had simply changed the constitution to suit their purposes. He could simply have stuck to his guns and weathered the storm.

As it turned out, he bowed to pressure – not from the people but from government and Establishment – and at 10am on 10 December, 1936, he signed the six copies of the Instrument of Abdication that were to lead to a lifetime of exile.

A King in Exile

Edward's brother Albert, who never thought he would be king, immediately became King George VI (1895–1952). Edward was given the title Duke of Windsor. He married Wallis in 1937, a year after her divorce. George VI told his brother that he could continue to be known as His Royal Highness, but neither his wife nor any children they might have would be entitled to receive the title. The couple went into exile and were largely shunned by the rest of the Royal Family – the late Queen Mother, it is said, never forgave Edward as she believed that her shy, stammering husband's life was shortened by the strain of being king.

Edward died in 1972, aged 78. Wallis outlived him by 14 years, ten of which were spent as a virtual recluse in their house in France where she died in

1986. She was buried beside Edward at Frogmore near Windsor, but even in death the scandalous couple were kept well away from the rest of the royal family, interred on the very edge of the burial ground.

Love Rats
James Hewitt and Co.

Scientists now think there may be a gene that causes some men to turn into what the tabloid newspapers describe as 'love rats'. A love rat can be an adulterer or better still a serial adulterer– in fact, anyone who cheats on their partner is a love rat, but of course it's only celebrities, the rich and the famous, whose ratting activities get the full tabloid treatment.

The most famous love rat has to be James Hewitt, the plummy ex-public schoolboy who was the lover of Diana, Princess of Wales for a period of some five years. Hewitt was bound to become the figure that the tabloids loved to hate once they discovered that he was trying to sell the love letters that had been written to him by Diana, the People's Princess, during their affair. The press vilified him for trying to make money out of his relationship with the beloved princess. Rather lamely, Hewitt responded that he just wanted to put the record straight – however, he wasn't about to hand the letters over free of charge!

The love rat label stuck – so much so that at one time Hewitt thought of living abroad to escape the barrage of newspaper stories.

But the papers took a purely commercial decision when they chose not to buy the letters – it wasn't that they were worried that buying the letters might be immoral; it was just that they felt they would gain more readers by not publishing. Given the popularity of the

RIGHT: THE TABLOID PRESS HAVE OFTEN QUESTIONED THE PARENTAGE OF PRINCE HARRY.

princess, it was a good bet that publication of such sensitive material might well have reduced rather than increased any tabloid's circulation.

Death of a Princess
Diana and Dodi

Was it just an accident? That was the question on everyone's lips after the strange death in a Paris underpass of Diana, Princess of Wales in 1997. Strange might seem an odd word to use but it's what springs to mind when we remember the rumours that surrounded the accident within hours of the news being flashed around the world.

At first there was the question of blame. Was it the driver of the Mercedes in which the princess and her lover, Dodi Fayed, were travelling who was to blame? An autopsy revealed high levels of alcohol in his blood which seemed to suggest that this might have been the main cause of the accident. But the family of the driver have disputed this and forensic evidence may have been contaminated.

The teams of photographers who took to their motorcycles that night in order to follow the princess were seen as the main culprits initially, only for the police to quickly drop all charges against them. And there were questions about the vehicle – why were the princess and Dodi not wearing their safety belts? Had they been strapped in they might well have survived – the only person in the car who did survive, bodyguard Trevor Rees Jones, did so precisely because he was wearing a safety belt. Why did the bodyguard not insist that all passengers – particularly the princess – wear safety belts?

All these questions led to massive speculation, none of which in the intervening years has either been proved or disproved. The scandal of the death of the princess continues to this day.

Conspiracy Theories

The main rumours that something untoward lies behind the death of Princess Diana stem from claims by Dodi Fayed's father, Mohamed al Fayed that his son was killed by the British security services because the British Establishment, particularly those close to the royal family, were terrified that Princess Diana might marry Dodi, the son of an Egyptian shopkeeper. The only way to make sure it didn't happen – so the conspiracy theorists would have us believe – was to make sure that Dodi and Diana were eliminated.

An official enquiry into the deaths found that the driver Henri Paul was entirely to blame simply because of the high levels of alcohol in his system, but like so many official enquiries this one was dismissed by many as a white-wash. Even those who dismiss the conspiracy theory point out that the driver would not have driven at such high speeds if he had not been pursued by a pack of paparazzi.

There is no doubt, too, that Diana was seen as something of a loose cannon by the British Establishment. She refused to stick to the bizarre rules of decorum and secrecy that most members of the royal family implicitly accept. Instead, she courted the media and spoke out about her private life and her emotional and marital crises. As her fame grew, she was, if anything, more likely to speak out more often and at greater length about her life in the royal inner circle – a prospect that must have been enormously worrying to the already much criticized royals.

Like so many scandals, the life and death of Diana, Princess of Wales is unlikely to go away.

Women Behaving Badly -
Madams and Mistresses

'Only those who risk going
too far can possibly find out
how far one can go.'

GEORGE ELIOT

The Somerset Bigamist
Mary Hamilton

Scandals in high places are only rarely matched by scandals lower down the social scale, but it would be difficult to find a more outrageous situation than one that was reported in newspapers in the West Country in 1746.

On 7 October of that year, a young countrywoman named Mary Hamilton was tried at Taunton Assizes for wrongfully marrying no fewer than 14 times. Bad enough one might say, but not only did Ms Hamilton marry 14 people – every last one of them was a woman! The last of the 14 wives appeared at the assizes to give evidence against Ms Hamilton, describing how they had been properly married in church, gone home to bed together and then lived happily as man and wife for three months. The wife then began to suspect that something was not quite right. Perhaps the oddest thing about the story is that this last wife seems to have been a little naïve about what exactly married couples are meant to do.

In court the complainant said that the 'vilest and the most deceitful practices' had been employed to mislead her. It is a pity that more precise details of these practices were not divulged to the court.

The judges got themselves in a fearful muddle when they tried to decide exactly what Mary Hamilton's sex really was. But they did establish that she operated under a string of aliases, including Charles Hamilton, George Hamilton and William Hamilton. Ultimately, they ruled that 'he, she, or whomsoever the prisoner at the bar, is an uncommon notorious cheat and is to be gaoled for six months during which time she is to be whipped in the towns of Taunton, Glastonbury, Wells and Shepton Mallet.' The sentence was duly carried out and hundreds turned up to watch the notorious bigamist being whipped on the very coldest days of winter.

The Travelling Eccentric
Lady Hester Stanhope

The entire life of Lady Hester Stanhope (1776–1839) seems to have been devoted to the sort of behaviour guaranteed to give her an appalling reputation among her contemporaries. In part this can be attributed to an inherent eccentricity. She spent much of her childhood, for example, hoping that it would rain so she could walk about on stilts to avoid the mud, and as a teenager she tried to row to France.

Despite her aristocratic birth, Stanhope was shunned by society for her devotion to what were considered exclusively masculine interests. She wanted

to travel alone, she shot and fished, she spoke her mind and refused to accept any restrictions based on her sex. From 1803, she worked for her uncle, William Pitt, the Prime Minister, giving him informal advice on a range of matters and acting as hostess at his parties. She was with him until his death in 1806, after which she received a pension of £1,200 a year. The sum was a fortune in the early 19th century and it enabled her to indulge her passion for travel.

The Queen of the East

In 1810, a patient at the notorious St Mary of Bethlehem mental hospital, otherwise known as Bedlam, told Stanhope that she would become Queen of the East, so she promptly set off for Jerusalem. Shipwrecked off Rhodes, she lost all her clothes and was forced to wear the local costume, but rather than wear women's clothes she chose the male dress of turban, loose trousers and a shirt. She refused thereafter to wear anything else. As she travelled east, her reputation spread far and wide. She was never molested, despite travelling through areas of the Middle East, such as Damascus, that were fiercely anti-Christian and deeply conservative in their attitude towards women. On the contrary, sheikhs travelled for miles across the desert to meet her.

After years of wandering, she finally settled at a disused monastery near Sidon in Lebanon. She became the de facto ruler over an enormous area and apparently wielded absolute authority over the natives. When a local warlord decided to invade Syria in 1832, he asked if she would mind remaining neutral in the coming conflict!

As the years passed, Stanhope became more reclusive, but when asked about this she simply said she was waiting for the prophecy to be fulfilled – the prophecy that said she would be crowned Queen of the East. Over the long years of waiting, she adopted the ways of the Middle East ever more enthusiastically, and learned to speak Arabic fluently. She explained her passion for the region by saying that she couldn't bear the English because they had flat feet. But she must have known that, such was the unusual nature of her adopted lifestyle, she could never return home.

By 1839, however, she had run out of money, having spent it all turning the derelict monastery into a sumptuous palace. With her fortune gone, she simply bricked up all the doors and windows and departed. A few months later she was dead. In her will she asked to be buried at midnight accompanied by the skull of one of her long-dead lovers with a candle burning in it. Even in death it seems she couldn't resist cocking a snook at convention.

The Prince's Vengeful Mistress
Mrs Clarke

London's Salisbury Square, just off Fleet Street, once witnessed the conclusion to one of the most bizarre disputes in the history of England. The problems began when the second son of George III, Frederick, Duke of York (1763–1827), began to lose interest in one of his mistresses, Mary Anne Clarke (1776–1852). Mrs Clarke was aggrieved that the Duke had lost interest in her, but she would have accepted this meekly enough if he had given her the pension she felt she deserved and a house in a fashionable part of London.

Frederick didn't pay up, so Mrs Clarke began to sell her influence – she promised those who paid her that she could gain military and ecclesiastical preferment for them. The scandal broke in 1809, when a Colonel Wardle, MP, brought charges of abuse of military patronage against the duke, forcing him to resign as Commander-in-Chief.

Still, Frederick refused to see Mrs Clarke or give her any money, so she sat down and wrote her memoirs in which she focused largely on her relationship with the prince. She had many letters that he had sent to her and these would certainly have been liberally sprinkled throughout the work. There is no doubt that the publisher she approached would have encouraged her to add as much juicy detail as possible to the book.

Mrs Clarke's notoriety and the public's appetite for scandal meant the publisher was convinced he would sell huge quantities and make his fortune. He printed 10,000 copies – an enormous number for any book at the time. Mrs Clarke then let the duke know that the book was about to be published. He immediately paid her a pension, found her a house and bought all 10,000 copies of the book – which were piled up in Salisbury Square and burned. If one copy had survived and were to turn up now it would be worth a fortune! The wily Mrs Clarke lived out the rest of her life on her pension.

The Notorious Novelist
George Eliot

Mary Ann Evans (1819–80) had to change her name to a man's, George Eliot, in order to pursue a successful career as a writer. The Victorians didn't see writing as a suitable occupation for a lady – respectable women were supposed to have babies, drink tea and sit delicately on a sofa. Better still, they should cultivate a sort of helpless physicality. Looking pale and frail was something that Victorian men found both respectable and sexually arousing. Respectable women were also supposed to be either married or single – they did not have lovers and certainly not married ones, which is why George Eliot found herself in deep trouble. Not only was she a fiercely intellectual writer, but she also lived with a man who was someone else's husband. The price she paid for following her own path and leading such a life was isolation. Eliot was effectively ostracized by all but a few friends, even though the man she lived with was considered perfectly respectable. It is ironic that what shocks us now is not the fact that Mary Ann lived with her lover, but that Victorian society was so hypocritical that it allowed him to do as he pleased while she was expected to conform.

Radical Mary

Mary Ann Evans was born in Warwickshire. Her father was a carpenter and she was educated largely at home. The family moved to Coventry where she came under the influence of the radical free thinker Charles Bray. At about the same

RIGHT: MARY ANN EVANS, AKA GEORGE ELIOT, WAS A STRONG-WILLED WOMAN, WHO REFUSED TO CONFORM TO VICTORIAN SOCIETY'S FEMININE IDEAL.

'When a woman's will is as strong as the man's who wants to govern her, half her strength must be concealment.'

George Eliot

time she began to lose her religious faith. After the death of her father in 1849, Evans travelled around Europe before settling in London where she worked on the *Westminster Review* and met George Henry Lewes (1817–78). By the 1850s she was living with Lewes, who was already married but separated.

It was during her time with Lewes, and she remained with him until his death, that Eliot wrote her greatest novels, from *Scenes of Clerical Life* (1858) to her masterpiece *Middlemarch* (1871–2). It may be that ostracism did George Eliot a favour – her isolation gave her time to write some of the greatest novels of the 19th century. In 1880, Eliot married the much younger John Walter Cross. In doing so, she regained some social standing, and was reunited with her beloved brother, who had so disapproved of her irregular life with Lewes.

Mistress of the Aristocracy
Catherine Walters

One of the most eccentric women of the 19th century was Catherine Walters (1839–1920); she is also proof that the power of personality can overcome almost any obstacle. Known as Skittles because she had a tiny waist, like a skittle, Walters was a great beauty. She was also one of a long line of professional courtesans. She lived her raucous life in an age that was probably the most moralistic – even if hypocritically so – in history. The Victorian obsession with purity and chastity, combined with the absolute rule of respectability meant that any middle- or working-class woman suspected of 'sexual irregularity' – as the Victorian newspapers might have put it – would be shunned by everyone. However, as always there was one rule for the general public and an entirely different rule for the elite.

Mrs Walters was the paid mistress of a number of members of the aristocracy, and when any of her various partners insisted upon it, society had to receive her. But even without aristocratic patronage, Skittles would have survived, as she seemed immune to the rules that applied to most people, simply because she didn't give a fig about them.

She was the mistress of both the Duke of Devonshire and the Marquess of Hartington, among others, and insisted on the finest clothes and carriages –

finer, it was said, than the wives of her lovers. Stories about her are legion. She loved horses and riding and when out with the Quorn Hunt in Leicestershire on one occasion she kept up with the leaders of the field until the fox was caught. The Master of Hounds ventured to compliment her on the fine, flushed colour of her cheeks. 'That's nothing,' she replied, 'you should see the colour of my ruddy arse!'

Walters lived for many years at No. 15 South Street in London – the house is still there – and in old age was pushed in her wheelchair through Hyde Park by none other than Lord Kitchener!

The Jersey Lily
Lillie Langtry

Born Emilie Charlotte Le Breton, Lillie Langtry (1852–1929) was the daughter of a Jersey vicar, and it is a testament to her energy and ambition that she went from such obscure beginnings to become one of the greatest celebrities of her day. But behind her public persona were numerous skeletons in cupboards – she was the mistress of a number of aristocrats, including Edward VII, and bore at least one illegitimate child.

Lillie was educated at home and was something of a tomboy, but in her late teens she revealed the determination that was to characterize her life when she married a 30-year-old Irish widower, Edward Langtry, and went to live with him on his yacht.

By 1876, the couple were living in London. What Lillie called her 'real life' began after a chance meeting with the Pre-Raphaelite painter John Everett Millais (1829–96) who asked if he could paint her. She had become hugely popular at social gatherings all over fashionable

RIGHT: LILLIE LANGTRY WAS THE MISTRESS OF TWO PRINCES AND AN ACCLAIMED BEAUTY.

London simply because of her beauty and wit, and when Millais' portrait of her was exhibited at the Royal Academy the crowds had to be held back to prevent the picture being damaged.

Legendary Beauty

Lillie Langtry's beauty was legendary – she was popularly known as the 'Jersey Lily'. By the late 1870s, she was the mistress of Edward, Prince of Wales, who had a house built at Bournemouth so that they could meet discreetly. Her husband apparently accepted her adultery, and the Princess of Wales had grown used to her husband's numerous affairs with prostitutes, servant girls and the wives of his friends and acquaintances.

Lillie knew that social and financial success depended on royal patronage, so she persuaded the prince to introduce her to Queen Victoria. After such an introduction, Lillie was invited everywhere. When Edward moved on to his next affair, Lillie found herself in the arms of Prince Louis of Battenberg (1854–1921), his cousin. She became pregnant with Louis's child and as soon as the royal family discovered this he was sent overseas with Lillie left to fend for herself. The scandal of her advancing pregnancy was resolved when she went anonymously to Paris to have the child. She was then advised – by Oscar Wilde, no less – to try her hand at acting, which she did with huge success. She later left for America where she was lionized. She made a fortune on the stage – enough, in fact, to buy a ranch. By 1887, she was a citizen of the United States and under American law was able to divorce Edward Langtry. She had numerous American lovers – they were always rich – and one gave her a 200-foot yacht as an apology for beating her up!

Lillie remarried at the age of 45 – her husband was 19 years her junior – but by then her wayward life was catching up with her. Her daughter by Louis Battenberg discovered that Edward Langtry was not her father. Outraged that she had been lied to, she refused to see her mother ever again. Lillie spent her last years at a villa in Monaco, where she died aged 75. She was never reconciled to her daughter and left all her money to her companion, Mathilda Peat, and nothing to her husband.

The Ultimate Royal Mistress
Mrs Keppel

The honourable Mrs George Keppel (1869–1947) led a life of the utmost scandal, yet she was never criticized or shunned by society, and during the period when she was most in the public eye – as Edward VII's mistress – she

Ph. Kirk et Sons.
Mistress Keppel

ABOVE: *ALICE KEPPEL, THE ULTIMATE ROYAL MISTRESS AND GREAT-GRANDMOTHER OF CAMILLA PARKER BOWLES.*

remained hugely popular with the general public. How on earth did she do it? The answer is discretion. She never complained, she was never jealous of Edward's other mistresses and she made a point of befriending Edward's wife and other members of his circle. Mrs Keppel also had the good fortune to have married a man who didn't seem in the least bit bothered what his wife got up to.

Mrs Keppel's skill, if skill it can be called, was to milk the system for as much as she could. Gifts and money flowed from Edward because she never nagged or embarrassed him – and she kept him happy. She amused him with her gossip and always found ways to sleep with him without being caught. All of Edward's friends and his wife knew that Mrs Keppel was his mistress, but it was never mentioned.

Playing By the Rules

Mrs Keppel was born Alice Frederica Edmonstone at Duntreath Castle on Loch Lomond. The castle and lands had been given to one of her ancestors in the 14th century by Robert III of Scotland. Alice grew up with a fine sense of the values – and hypocrisies – of the aristocracy; she knew the rules of the game instinctively and played them as well as it was possible to play them. The big problem for Alice was money. The family had very little, despite their grand houses and estate. When she married Lord George Keppel in 1891, her financial situation did not improve; although he was well connected, Keppel was also poor.

The couple moved to London and, as the Keppels had a tradition of service to the crown, it wasn't long before they were dining regularly with circles close to the Prince of Wales. Alice wanted money – her daughter recalled that all her life Alice wanted to be close to bank managers – and as George could not provide this she was determined to find someone who could.

Her affair with Edward began in 1898, when he was still Prince of Wales. He was 58 and she was 29. She was statuesque and very attractive; he was extremely overweight –he weighed more than 16 stone – and just five feet seven inches tall. He also smoked and coughed continually, but what he lacked in physical qualities, he made up for in position and wealth and that was what Mrs Keppel exploited.

By the time Edward died in 1910, Mrs Keppel was hugely wealthy and able to lead a life of luxury in her houses in England and abroad. But her relationship with the king is said to have ruined her daughter Violet's life. Violet, who was probably Edward's child, hated the deception and duplicity of it all. What made it worse was that, as a lesbian, she was forced to adopt the same tactics of discretion she so loathed in her mother in order to keep her various lovers a secret.

One of the curious things about Mrs Keppel, the ultimate royal mistress, is that she was the great-grandmother of another royal adulteress – Mrs Camilla Parker Bowles.

The Battling Suffragettes
The Pankhursts

It is difficult now to understand the shockwaves that the suffragette movement created in the last part of the 19th century and the early part of the 20th century. What is even odder is that large numbers of those who didn't want votes for women were women themselves!

It was strongly felt by many that women taking part in the political process would somehow undermine the traditional female roles of home-maker and mother. It was also likely to undermine the Victorian male's ideal of a woman as a frail and child-like creature whose perfection would be damaged by too much contact with the outside world. Leader writers in the newspapers, clergy-men and bishops, MPs and captains of industry – all of whom were, of course, men – fulminated against the suffragette movement.

A Female Voice

The movement began in 1897 when Millicent Fawcett (1847–1929) founded the National Union of Women's Suffrage. Fawcett argued that if the laws made in parliament affected women, then women should have some say in how those laws were made and by whom. She was committed to the idea of peace-ful, rational campaigning, but by 1903 a group of more radical women decided that they were fed up with waiting. The Women's Social and Political Union was founded by the most famous suffragettes of all – Emmeline Pankhurst (1859–1928) and her daughters Christabel (1880–1961) and Sylvia (1882–1960). These women were not prepared to stick to non-violent methods of protest and began a long and bitter battle with the government.

Political meetings were interrupted by banner-waving women, churches were burned down – the Church, reactionary as always, was firmly against votes for women – and shop windows were smashed. The suffragettes then began chaining themselves to railings, including those at Buckingham Palace. As a result of such militancy they were imprisoned and went on hunger strike. It was at this point that the government of Herbert Asquith decided to put its foot down. They tried to force feed the hunger strikers, but this caused a public outcry. The women were therefore allowed to remain on hunger strike until they were seriously weakened, at which point they were released. As soon as they'd recovered sufficiently to begin campaigning again they were promptly re-arrested and thrown back into prison.

In 1913 the suffragettes' campaign resulted in two unprecedented acts: the blowing up of part of David Lloyd George's house and the death of Emily Wilding Davison, who threw herself under the king's horse, Anmer, at the Derby.

The suffragette movement was suspended during the First World War, but women were finally enfranchised in 1918 through the Representation of the People Act. Even then the vote was only given to women over 30 who owned property. Women didn't achieve full and equal voting rights with men until 1928.

Sisters Opposed – Nazis and Communists
The Mitfords

By any standards, the Mitfords were an extraordinary family. Anyone who has read Nancy Mitford's semi-autobiographical novels *Love in a Cold Climate* and *The Pursuit of Love* will realize just how eccentric an upbringing the six sisters had in their gloomy old house in Oxfordshire with no formal education and eccentric parents.

Certainly, their childhood produced an extraordinary outcome. Nancy (1904–73), was, of course, a celebrated novelist; Pamela (1907–94), was the quiet sister who shunned the limelight; Diana (1910–2004) married one of the most controversial political figures of her generation; Unity (1914–48) was an ardent disciple of Adolf Hitler; Jessica (1917–96) was a Communist and Deborah (born 1920) became the mistress of Chatsworth House in Derbyshire. Needless to say, it was the political sisters who most attracted attention to themselves.

Fame and Fascism

Diana, a celebrated beauty, was the first to court controversy. She had married a rich member of the Guinness family, but when she met Oswald Mosley (see pages 152–4), she dropped everything, leaving her husband and two small sons. She had a very open affair with Mosley, and married him in 1936 in the presence of Hitler and Goebbels. Mosley had formed the British Union of

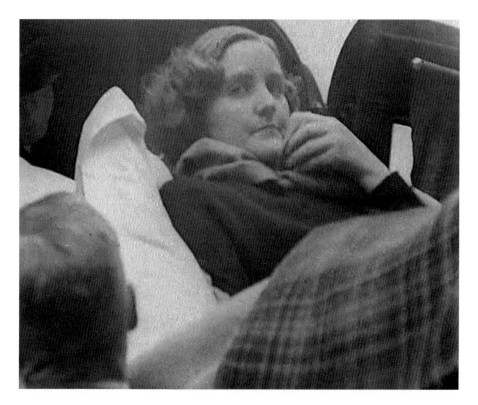

ABOVE: *U*NITY *M*ITFORD *ATTEMPTED SUICIDE ON HEARING THE NEWS THAT* *G*REAT *B*RITAIN *HAD DECLARED WAR ON HER BELOVED* *N*AZI *G*ERMANY.

Fascists, which Diana heartily supported. She defended fascism and her husband's beliefs for the rest of her life. As late as the 1980s, she was still insisting that although Hitler might have been a bit beastly, he nevertheless had very good manners and lovely eyes. During the Second World War (1939–45), Diana and Oswald Mosley were arrested and imprisoned. Nancy Mitford went on record as saying that she thought her sister's views more dangerous than her brother-in-law's.

Diana's younger sister, Unity, was also a passionate supporter of Hitler and his politics. She was so distraught when Britain declared war on Germany in 1939 that she attempted suicide by shooting herself in the head. However, she made a bad job of it and survived as a semi-invalid for a number of years afterwards.

Civil War and Communism

Meanwhile, Jessica Mitford – or Decca as she was always known – became an ardent socialist, accompanying her first husband Esmond Romilly to Europe to fight in the Spanish Civil War. Romilly disappeared, and when Decca later tried to find out what had happened to him, she asked a family friend, who just happened to be Winston Churchill, to investigate. Churchill confirmed that Esmond was indeed dead (killed when his plane came down over the Atlantic Ocean), but he tried to comfort Decca by telling her that her sister, Diana, was being made as comfortable as conditions in prison would allow! Not that she would have cared – Decca hated her older sister and everything she stood for.

Jessica emigrated to America in 1939, where she became a committed Communist, appearing at just about every important left-wing picket line and demonstration for more than 40 years. She also wrote a number of what she liked to refer to as 'muck-raking' books, including *The American Way of Death*. Decca campaigned for black civil rights in the 1950s and on one occasion was barricaded in a church with Martin Luther King while an angry mob bayed for their blood outside.

The Last Woman Hanged
Ruth Ellis

The execution of Ruth Ellis in Holloway Prison, London, in 1955 so scandalized the public's sense of fair play that her death became a key factor in the abolition of the death penalty a decade later in 1965.

Ellis, a bar manager from Kensington, had become infatuated with David Blakeley, with whom she had a tempestuous affair. Blakeley seems to have

spent his life drinking, repairing old cars and occasionally beating Ruth up – she once miscarried after he punched her in the stomach.

Both Blakeley and Ellis were unfaithful to each other during their relationship, but Ellis could not bear to lose him completely. When he

LEFT: *RUTH ELLIS WAS GUILTY OF A CRIME OF PASSION, WHICH SHE PAID FOR WITH HER LIFE.*

refused to see her over a period of several weeks in 1955, she got hold of a gun and went to the Magdala Pub in Hampstead, where he drank regularly. It was Easter Sunday. She waited until he appeared outside the hostelry and then shot him once. He tried to escape by running around his car, but she followed him, fired again and then, as he lay on the ground, she continued firing until the gun was empty. With six bullets in him, all fired from close range, Blakeley died almost immediately.

Ruth Ellis was arrested by an off-duty policeman at the scene. At her trial she accepted her guilt with equanimity, hardly bothering to put together a defence. She was found guilty and sentenced to death. The Home Secretary refused to commute her sentence to life imprisonment. She went to the gallows on the morning of 13 July 1955. Albert Pierrepont, Britain's last public executioner, pulled the pin that released the trapdoor under her feet and Ruth Ellis plummeted to oblivion.

Huge crowds had gathered outside the prison the night before her death to protest at the killing. Tens of thousands of signatures had been collected on various petitions and presented to parliament, but none of it was effective. From the public's point of view, Ellis had committed a crime of passion, which many thought should have been taken into account. Ellis was also the mother of two young children. Other individuals who had committed murder with far less provocation had done their time and been released, but Ellis had refused to play the court's game. She insisted throughout that having taken a life she deserved to lose her own.

Madam Cyn
Cynthia Payne

Cynthia Payne, the Streatham Madam, became a celebrity after she appeared in court in 1980 charged with running 'a disorderly house' – the legal euphemism for running a brothel. What endeared Ms Payne to the public was her no-nonsense attitude to her profession. She insisted on keeping her suburban villa clean and tidy, provided food, tea, condoms and comfortable bedrooms and accepted luncheon vouchers in return for sex. She insisted she couldn't understand what all the fuss was about – for her sex was just like having a cup of tea.

The court was outraged and sentenced her to 18 months in prison, which was reduced on appeal. When a book about her life was published she sent the judge a signed copy with the message: 'I hope this will broaden your outlook as you've obviously led a very sheltered life.'

ABOVE: CYNTHIA PAYNE'S DOWN-TO-EARTH ATTITUDE TO SEX MADE HER A FAVOURITE WITH THE GENERAL PUBLIC.

What many people loved about Cynthia Payne – described by her biographer as a 'chirpy cockney woman going round telling people to behave themselves' – was the fact that she was so down-to-earth about her profession, as is illustrated in this quotation from an interview given after she was acquitted:

'I have known clients who liked sweaty women. I once had one who asked for a girl who hadn't washed under her armpits for a month. He said that's what turned him on.... Well, we always tried our best, and I always wanted my customers to leave satisfied, but how could I possibly ask a girl not to wash under her armpits for a whole month? In the end, we compromised, and she didn't wash for three days. I think he was reasonably satisfied, and probably paid her a bit extra.'

Ms Payne was also nostalgic about the business in the good old days, as she explained:

'In my day, we did it the proper way – £25 without extras, food and drink, and a choice of ladies. We knocked off £5 for old age pensioners and we charged men half-price if they were past it and just fancied watching.

'We had a high-class clientèle – no rowdy kids, no yobs, all well-dressed men in suits, who knew how to respect a lady. You had to be at least 45 to come to one of my parties. It was like a vicar's tea party with sex thrown in.'

Terry Jones, the former Monty Python star who directed *Personal Services*, the film about Cynthia Payne's life, was a witness for the defence when she was charged with running a disorderly house. He described her parties as genial – a lot of elderly, lonely people drinking sherry. Despite the loss of her business, Cynthia Payne found a new career: 'These days I am still in demand – but in a different way. In my 30s I was doing it, in my 40s I was organizing it and now unfortunately I can only talk about it!'

INDEX

PICTURE ACKNOWLEDGEMENTS

The Bridgeman Art Library: Plate 17.
Chris Coe: Page 18.
Getty Images: Front cover top left; Pages 86, 112, 165; Plates 9, 15, 20.
The Illustrated London News: Pages 71, 72, 151, 209; Plate 21.
ITN Archive Stills: Front cover, centre; Spine; Pages 74, 75, 78, 90, 107,
116, 153, 157, 159, 160, 167, 173, 193, 195, 211, 212, 214; Plates 8,
19.
Mary Evans Picture Library: Pages 23, 35, 40, 47, 51, 82, 201, 207; Plates
1, 3, 10, 18.
Mary Evans/Harry Price: Front cover, centre left; Plate 4.
National Portrait Gallery, London: Page 76.
The National Trust/Angelo Hornak: Page 14.
Courtesy of Christine Sloane/Photographer: Lewis Morley/Akehurst Gallery:
Front cover, top right.
Time Life Pictures/Getty Images: Page 57.
Courtesy of University College London Special Collections: Page 43.